'There is nothing ambiguous about ... nveys.
Hailed as Britain's most accurate medium.' **The Daily Mail**

'Gordon Smith is down-to-earth about his heavenly talents.'
The Sunday Telegraph magazine

'You don't meet men like Gordon Smith every day - he's the Psychic
Barber who never needs to ask where you're going on holiday.'
The Scotsman

'It's impossible not to warm to Gordon Smith. He is one of the country's
most successful mediums.' **Daily Express**

'Gordon's gift was to soothe the grief of the heartbroken,
to give them hope.' **The Guardian**

'Amazing' **Time Out**

'There's no doubt for me he's the real deal. His accuracy had the hairs
standing up on the back of my neck.' **Woman's Own**

'Top medium and TV phenomenon Gordon Smith astounds countless
people with his messages from the other side.'
Spirit & Destiny magazine

'Gordon Smith provides exact names, addresses, events and descriptions
sharply relevant to a person's life and the lives of those they have known.'
**Professor Archie E. Roy, Emeritus Professor of Astronomy,
Glasgow University**

'The talent Gordon has been blessed with is something most of us can
hardly believe, but to see and hear of the help he has given to others in
easing their pain is surely his greatest gift.' **Ally McCoist**

Through My Eyes

Hay House Titles of Related Interest

Books

Adventures of a Psychic, by Sylvia Browne
Angel Therapy, by Doreen Virtue, Ph.D.
Chakra Clearing, by Doreen Virtue, Ph.D.
Conversations with the Other Side, by Sylvia Browne
Crossing Over, by John Edward
Diary of a Psychic, by Sonia Choquette
Daily Guidance from your Angels, by Doreen Virtue
David Well's Complete Guide to Developing Your Psychic Skills
Healing with the Angels, by Doreen Virtue
If You Could See What I See, by Sylvia Browne
Spirit & Destiny Soul Secrets
Trust Your Vibes, by Sonia Choquette

Card Decks

Archangel Oracle Cards, by Doreen Virtue, Ph.D.
Healing with the Angels Oracle Cards, by Doreen Virtue, Ph.D.
Messages from your Angels Oracle Cards, by Doreen Virtue, Ph.D.
Ask Your Guides, by Sonia Choquette
Trust Your Vibes Oracle Cards, by Sonia Choquette

All of the above are available at your local bookshop,
or may be ordered by visiting:
Hay House UK: www.hayhouse.co.uk
Hay House USA: www.hayhouse.com
Hay House Australia: www.hayhouse.com.au
Hay House South Africa: orders@psdprom.co.za

Through My Eyes
Gordon Smith

HAY HOUSE

Australia • Canada • Hong Kong
South Africa • United Kingdom • United States

Published and distributed in the United Kingdom by:
Hay House UK Ltd, 292B Kensal Road, London W10 5BE
Phone: (44) 20-8962-1230 • *Fax:* (44) 20-8962-1239 • www.hayhouse.co.uk

Published and distributed in the United States by:
Hay House, Inc., P.O. Box 5100, Carlsbad, CA 92018-5100
Phone: (1) 760-431-7695 or (1) 800-654-5126
Fax: (1) 760-431-6948 or (1) 800-650-5115 • www.hayhouse.com

Published and distributed in Australia by:
Hay House Australia Ltd, 18/36 Ralph St., Alexandria NSW 2015
Phone: (61) 2-9669-4299 • *Fax:* (61) 2-9669-4144 • www.hayhouse.com.au

Published and distributed in the Republic of South Africa by:
Hay House SA (Pty) Ltd, P.O. Box 990, Witkoppen 2068
Phone/Fax: (27) 11-706-6612 • orders@psdprom.co.za

Published and distributed in India by:
Hay House Publishers India, Muskaan Complex, Plot No.3, B-2,
Vasant Kunj, New Delhi – 110 070.
Phone: (91) 11 41761620 • *Fax:* (91) 11 41761630 • contact@hayhouseindia.co.in

Distributed in Canada by:
Raincoast, 9050 Shaughnessy St., Vancouver, B.C. V6P 6E5
Phone: (1) 604-323-7100 • *Fax:* (1) 604-323-2600

© Gordon Smith, 2006, 2007

A catalogue record for this book is available from the British Library

Design: Leanne Siu

ISBN 978-1-4019-1525-4

Printed and bound in Great Britain by TJ International, Padstow, Cornwall.

Contents

Acknowledgements   viii

Preface   ix

Chapter 1: Through the Darkness   1

Chapter 2: Lost in Grief   9

Chapter 3: Truth Hurts   33

Chapter 4: Realising Life Beyond Death   55

Chapter 5: Why They Come Back   79

Chapter 6: Messages of Hope   107

Chapter 7: How We Die   117

Chapter 8: Jewels of the Mind   135

Chapter 9: Healing Life and Death   165

Chapter 10: First Contact   189

Chapter 11: Messages of Love   211

Chapter 12: A Celebration of Life   225

Chapter 13: Bringing Comfort   249

Chapter 14: Spiritual Joy   259

Also Available by Gordon Smith   267

Dedication

To Cheeky Charlie – more than just a dog.

Acknowledgements

I would like to thank Reid Tracy for believing in me. Grateful thanks also to Michelle Pilley for all her great inspiration, and to Megan Slyfield and Jo Lal for always being so solid.

Thank you to Nancy Levene for looking after me so well. And special thanks to Susanna Forrest for her excellent work in editing.

As always, thank you to all my family, and to my good friend Gordon Gunn.

Preface

The DVD included in the back of this edition of *Through My Eyes* was recorded at one of my Evenings of Mediumship in 2006. It is my firm hope that this DVD will give *all* of you – not just those of you who were there – the chance to see that our loved ones' existence does not end at the point of death.

I truly hope this will bring comfort and reassurance that there is life after death -- that you really cannot die for the life of you.

Peace be with you,

Gordon Smith

CHAPTER ONE

Through the Darkness

Through the Darkness

Lots of people think that being a medium is just about talking to the dead, and dealing with all kinds of spooky things like ghosts and poltergeists, but I know after 18 years of working as one and giving sittings for thousands of people around the world, that my contribution is really about healing the living. I have worked as a healer with people who have physical health problems, but that's not what I mean. The ultimate healing a medium can offer is to those who have lost someone they loved, and who they felt meant more to them than life itself.

I'm trying to lift the bereaved out of the fear, anger and sadness that crowd their every thought, and not only to help them overcome those in their daily lives, but also to show them that there is another life beyond death – a life after life, if you like.

Death is only part of our journey, and it comes to all of us, yet most people choose not to recognize that fact. It may be painful to face death, but not to accept it means being completely deluded. It's strange to me how far people will go to avoid thinking about it, because they truly believe that their consciousness will be snuffed out forever in an instant.

I've been in contact with the conscious life force, or Spirit, for most of my life, and because of my experiences I see death not as an end but as a new beginning. Our existence after death is one which is brighter and freer than the one we know in this life, and in this book I'd like to try to explain what that means, and how we have nothing to fear in dying, nor in losing a loved one.

Death affects each person in a different way. There does not seem to be any rhyme or reason to human behaviour when death touches us. Some whom we regard as being pillars of strength dissolve, while others whom we'd thought of as weak become stoic. I remember a medium I worked with who fell apart when her husband died, even though she had been comforting the bereaved for many years and had received confirmation of life after death time and time again. It seemed that she couldn't move on and kept trying to get messages from him from other mediums.

Those who accept death as a part of existence move through their bereavement more easily than those who see it as a catastrophe they never expected. That's not to say that they won't still have moments when a vivid memory will move them to tears, but this is part of the natural course of grief, and can, with time, become a more positive experience.

It is not death, or grief, which is complicated, but people and our behaviour. Every death we endure is different, and comes with a unique set of emotional meanings and triggers for each person who knew the deceased. The way we handle a loss also depends on our circumstances at the time, and while at one stage in our life we may be able to cope with parting from someone we were very close to, at another time we might be more vulnerable and break down.

The suffering which a person goes through is caused by the feeling of disconnection. When someone they were so closely bonded to in life is no longer in their sight, and cannot be touched, heard, or smelled, they are left with a feeling of being cut off forever. Memories of the things that they went through together seem diminished because they can no longer be shared.

This feeling is the first in a line of experiences of fear which we all go through in our grieving process. We are reminded too that we are vulnerable to death as are our children, family and friends. Grieving can become a sort of mental solitary confinement which crushes hope and leads to despair and depression, but there is a path through the darkness, for those who try to follow it.

I would never belittle someone's loss or expect them to be philosophical and just pick up the pieces of their life and move on, as grief is a powerful, devastating experience and permanently alters your being. However, sometimes people make the burden of grief much greater for themselves, and an already gruelling process becomes almost impossible.

When the bereaved come for sittings I get a tremendous sense of a sort of heavy emotional blanket that is both weighing them down and blocking out the light that is there to be seen. The worse their convictions, the heavier the blanket becomes and the harder to lift. I try to pull away and understand the layers of that depression and to move them toward an acceptance of their loss and steer them away from death toward life. Until these people see that they are only trapping themselves and holding themselves back, they will not be able to function as human beings and reclaim their lives. I hope this book can help in that process.

At this moment in time so many people need answers to the big questions, and many of them are turning to mediums. It could just be that everything is happening as it should and we are merely becoming a little more compassionate and are reaching out for spiritual enlightenment. Or maybe it's because the world is in such a state of upheaval, with wars and random terrorist attacks, violent storms and massive natural disasters. We are seeing people dying in unthinkable numbers, and so it only makes sense that we're all looking for the hope of an afterlife. It's rather like the era of the two World Wars, when spiritualism was at its peak, and people flocked to mediums in order to find evidence that their loved ones were still with them.

Whatever it is that's causing this upsurge in interest in mediums, it's making people look deeper into themselves, their lives and their purpose on this earth, and that cannot be a bad thing.

The world is certainly changing and more people are becoming interested in and open about their thoughts and beliefs.

This book is my take on such things – which comes out of my own experiences and the stories people have passed on to me. I hope that if you are struggling with grief yourself, or know someone who is in that dark place, you can find something that helps you here. I've tried to offer all sorts of advice, from the spiritual to the practical, from how to go about visiting a medium to how to arrange a funeral.

There's just one note before you start. Whenever I give a sitting I make sure that I know nothing about the folk who are coming to see me – that's standard procedure in all good Spiritualist organisations. It helps to make sure that the reading the person gets is influenced only by the Spirit world, and not by the medium's own guesses. As I show in Chapter Seven, sometimes there are clues you can't avoid picking up, but I could never fabricate the accurate information I am able to give people.

CHAPTER TWO

Lost in Grief

Lost in Grief

In these next two chapters I want to write about the various ways people get lost in grief and, later on, look at the Spirit's experience of passing over, and how, if we comprehend that, we might find our bereavement easier to bear. In the years of meeting people as a medium, I've seen people torture themselves with the same misconceptions again and again.

'Torture' is the right word; there is a very real sense in which those left behind think of the dead as suffering, and think that they too should be in pain. They loved them and did not want to see them go through terrible things, so they try to take some of that agony onto themselves. They want to hurt because if they are hurting they believe they are closer to their loved ones, and maybe they will lighten their burden on the other side. They think constantly of the one they have lost and lose interest in the present, which is a world in which they think their loved ones have no part.

I see this most often with mothers who have lost children of any age. Their love is so strong and their sense of responsibility so absolute that they want to go where they think their children are. They imagine that the child is still suffering and put themselves in the same place mentally and spiritually. They blame themselves for not being able to protect their son or daughter from whatever it was that they died of – a sickness or an accident.

The need to punish themselves is so strong that people will even pick out things that they could never have done differently and worry themselves sick about them. I've lost track of the number of times people tell me 'I never got to say goodbye', especially after a sudden death, as though they should have known that they would lose their loved one. To linger over that is to beat yourself up needlessly as the past is not something you can change, only come to terms with.

I recently saw a man who had lost his daughter at the age of 19. He came with his wife, who was the girl's stepmother, and who was at the end of her tether. The family's attempts to draw him out of his mourning just made him think they were trying to take his daughter from him all over again. It had been eighteen months since the teenager, Helen, had died, but he had immersed himself so deeply in grief that his wife could no longer reach him. Every day he went to Helen's grave to take flowers and talk to her. He had tried to kill himself several times, to the horror of those around him.

Some of his behaviour came from the manner of his daughter's passing. She'd become very ill, very quickly, and he had taken her to hospital, only to be turned away as the doctors believed she was not in danger. The next day she was worse and the man had driven her to the hospital again, only for the tests to conclude that she was essentially all right. The day after that she died of what had turned out to be meningitis, undiagnosed until it was too late to help her.

None of this was her father's fault, but in his love for her and desperate grief he truly believed it was and he was doing a penance that took a heavy toll not only on him but also on his family. His daughter came through at the sitting very swiftly and gave me plenty of evidence to give to the couple – her name, her age, the day she'd died and what had happened to her.

She was also furious with her father for what he was doing; she was very clear that she did not need him to go to her grave every day as, she spelt out, 'I am not there. You are making a shrine to a carcass. You need to see that I am dead and you will never hold me or be able to cuddle me again.' She wanted him to see that her consciousness lived on and was not confined to her body, 'Start to think of me in a different light as I am still around you.' She thought he was trying to make her into some kind of saintly being that she'd never been in life, and began to list plenty of times in life when she had been less than a good girl.

When the man's wife backed this up, he turned on her,

unable to stand anything negative being said about his beloved Helen. I continued to convey the messages from Helen, though, and she was a straight talker. 'I knew you as a happy man, has my death killed you? When did you last laugh?' she insisted. Even then the man fought against the truth, but finally she said something that jolted him out of the dark place where he'd cornered himself.

'I can't reach you when you are like this. You have gone too deeply into yourself and I know how to get to my father, but I don't know how to get to you because you are not my father.' At this the man's expression changed. The moment he realized he was cutting his daughter off was the moment he found a different kind of responsibility to her in death – by putting an end to the hurt he was turning on himself, Helen and his wife, he would find himself closer to the real child he thought he had lost. He could keep her alive not by haunting her grave but by remembering her as she really was.

At the end of the sitting I really felt as though he would leave that room as, not a new man, but as the old dad Helen remembered – the one who had made her laugh and loved her for all her faults. His wife looked as though a weight had fallen from her shoulders too when they made their goodbyes, and I hoped they could get back to some sort of normality now.

It was no surprise to me that the man's whole attitude which had seemed so fixed was so quickly transformed. In twenty or so years working to try to reconnect the bereaved to those they have lost I have seen thousands of cases where the understanding that the Spirit lives on has lifted people out of a sort of cocoon of depression into which they have retreated.

This is the real reason why the Spirits return to give proof that they have survived death. They do not want to see us in pain and sometimes it needs a direct message from the other side to make that dramatic mental shift.

I met Joyce Dixon for the first time for an appointment at the Spiritualist Association of Great Britain in Belgrave Square, London. The SAGB invites mediums on a regular basis to take one-to-one readings with those in need, who can book in and take pot luck as to which practitioner they see. They won't know in advance whom they'll be assigned, and we mediums have no idea who will walk through the door of the little room next. That day it was Joyce.

She was a small woman, very thin and frail-looking. Her eyes were deep-set and almost black, and her short brown and grey hair lay limply round her small face. She looked to me on first impression as though she'd gone to hell and back and had stopped caring for herself.

When I looked straight into her eyes it was as though there was a deep chasm behind them, but I convinced myself that somewhere in that void was a spark of hope, and I knew that for some reason she was pinning a lot on the reading I was about to give. The session began as usual with me explaining what may or may not happen, and then I took her hand and said a silent prayer that I'd be able to help her in some way. A voice came through immediately, saying, 'Tell her it was me who made her turn on the telly.' Usually I'd ask for a name to go with the voice, but this time I just repeated the communication directly to Joyce. Her eyes widened, but she said nothing. Then the voice added, 'I came to her in a dream.' Again, her expression was all in her eyes. Then I gave her the name Marty, and Joyce smiled and cried all at the same time.

The next few things that came through didn't have any sort of special meaning for me, but I could tell that they were striking chords every time for Joyce. Marty said he was glad that Joyce had not been to see him in the morgue. He added a few more details to build the proof that it was really he who was in touch.

Then he said something that to me summed up the nature of the bond between those who have passed over and those who are left behind. He had had, he said, many chances to progress in the afterlife, but he knew that his mother was still devastated at losing him and that he had to help her before he could do that. He also explained that as she became lighter of mind, so did he.

The more I passed on to Joyce, the more I could see her mood lift, and that had a powerful effect on Marty's messages too – the communication was to me, as a medium, clearer and stronger. He reminded his mother of all sorts of scrapes he'd got into as a child, and she brightened so much that she actually laughed out loud. They were working as a team again – and the love they shared was reinvigorating both the mother and the son in Spirit. The last part of his message was simple and yet deeply meaningful to his mum – he thanked her for her prayers and said that they were working.

At the end of the sitting Joyce and I spoke for over an hour about her son's life and she explained the evidence he had given her. Marty had died in a car crash and she had been unable to face identifying his body when it had been so broken. She had been pitched into a state of shock that she saw no way out of, and just ceased to be able to communicate with her husband and her other children, no matter how well-meaning their words and actions were.

She had been, she told me, dead on the outside and she'd thought that as long as she felt that way, she was with the son who had gone out one day and never come home to her. She knew instinctively that he was not gone, but still connected to her, but every time she thought about him she could only imagine his injuries and think of the way he'd died. Hiding from that horror drove her deeper into herself and away from happier memories.

She fixated on the fact that she had left her husband to go to the morgue alone, and in her confusion felt guilty for not being there. It was a way of taking some of the blame for his death and justifying some of the pain she was now going through.

She didn't sleep properly for months, but one night she drifted off in her armchair. She found herself dreaming of Marty holding her and talking to her and his presence was so vivid that she could smell him – a scent so familiar to her that it made her sit up and call out his name. She woke with tears running down her face and a desperate need to be back in that dream where her son was so close.

As she tried frantically to run back over the dream and burn it into her memory she suddenly recalled something he had said – of all things, that she should turn on the television. She hadn't had any interest in doing such a thing for months, obviously, but now she pushed the on button. She picked up the remote to raise the volume and found herself avidly watching.

The programme showed a medium giving messages to a husband and wife from Yorkshire who had lost a son in a car crash a few months previously. As she watched the couple Joyce began to cry for them, as she knew exactly what they had experienced. When the documentary ended Joyce decided that the dream she had had must somehow have come from Marty – it was the first time since his death that she had felt truly alive – and if she knew that to be true, then she believed that he was trying to tell her that he too could communicate to her via a medium like the boy on the television.

That revelation was what had led her to the SAGB that afternoon and the messages from Marty. The documentary was part of the BBC's Everyman series and I had been the medium helping the couple. Marty had directed her very precisely to the person he thought would enable him to break through to her and draw her out of that living death into which she'd fallen.

When Joyce left she turned and thanked me for what she called a 'healing' and that must have been absolutely what Marty intended for her. He had certainly engineered things so that his mother would have confirmation of what she had, in some small part of her, known all along – that he did not die in that wrecked car, but was still with her.

I've written before that I believe that you cannot die for the life of you and I truly think that everyone knows that instinctively, just as Joyce did. It's when you deny that continued existence that grief closes in and becomes suffocating. In doing that you cut a part of yourself off and try to shut it away once and for all, and it is as though it died with the loved one.

You may feel divided from them by death, but it's a veil that can easily be lifted. Just because you can no longer touch or hear them it does not mean that you cannot feel their presence and the way they live on in so many things and people around you. It's not a belief that is easy for people to accept because it is often dismissed as wishful thinking or delusion, but for those who have had incontrovertible evidence that their beloved friend or relative still exists, that knowledge brings immeasurable comfort.

One day a few years ago when I was working at my hairdressing salon, I got a call from a friend who reads tarot. She asked what time I finished work and if I would come and speak to someone who had come to her for a reading. Tarot isn't the same thing as mediumship, so I asked her why she needed me. She explained that a man had come to visit her thinking that she would be able to contact someone on the other side for him. Obviously she couldn't, and he appeared to be so troubled by seeing someone who was happy to call herself a witch that he was very worked up. She thought he needed help immediately.

I had just finished my last appointment so I told her I'd be there as soon as I could. My friend worked in a room decked out with all sorts of symbols of arcana – crystal balls, swords, candles – not the kind of simple, neutral room where I prefer to do mediumship if I can help it, and the man looked extremely uncomfortable in such a setting.

I sat down opposite him and tried to go over what would

happen and what I would try to do, and he scarcely looked any more at ease. I expect he thought we were a bunch of fraudsters and that I was about to pretend to go into trance and start babbling about being his long-lost Auntie June. Something had compelled him to see the whole thing through, though, and he grimly sat tight as I tuned into the Spirit world.

A lady came through who said she was his wife. At first he didn't want to accept the evidence, even when she gave me her name. Then as she threw out more and more stories and little details I saw that he couldn't reason himself out of believing that it really was her any more. He started to cry, and once he'd begun he couldn't stop. The news that came through many times in his wife's communication was that she was with Jesus now – she was very clear about this, and it finally sank into his consciousness too.

As I carried on with the sitting he confessed between sobs that he was a Church of Scotland minister – not the kind of person who should have been sitting in a study lined with books on the occult! I tried to console him and he went on to say, 'I never really believed it. All these years I've been standing there at the front of the church telling everyone about the afterlife and I never once believed it! Not until now.' When his wife died he had been so devastated that he thought his prayers had gone unanswered and despite his faith he had thought the worst – that her soul had ceased to be.

He was shaken when he left, but reaffirmed not only in his love for his wife but also in his religious calling. I think this just goes to show how cruel death can seem and how hard it can be to see beyond it, even for those whose life-long beliefs point the way.

In all the communications I have passed from the Spirit world I have never heard of anyone being punished on the other side, or judged by anything other than their own conscience. Once our Spirit has cleared the physical and mental states that drive our behaviour on earth – those things that lead us to be greedy, selfish or jealous – it expands and is no longer restricted or harmed by those petty emotions.

Without a body there are none of the needs or desires for sensual pleasures which make us act so badly toward one another. We don't need to control others or strike out at them. Some take longer to reach this first stage of spiritual enlightenment than others, but we are all headed in that direction.

I have been told by so many Spirit beings that they at some point arrive at an understanding of their life and its purpose, where they accept all actions which they carried out, good and bad. They realize how limited they were in the physical state and how restricting they were to others, all because of their human emotions. Those who get stuck between life and death will remain so until they accept their own freedom from the weight of their own conscience.

You don't find this version of the afterlife in many religious books, and it's no wonder that many don't want to face the realities of death when you consider all the myths about what happens to us when we die. I have seen many people who were distraught because they thought their loved ones were now in limbo, or, worse still, undergoing horrendous torments in some hell realm.

We struggle with imagery of judgement and fire and brimstone, or with perfect angelic beings that humans could never measure up to, and it turns death into a punishment for the living. It's no wonder people try to avoid thinking about what will happen to them when they die and then crumble when they lose someone and imagine them at the mercy of all kinds of forces and themselves powerless to help them.

That's why the Spirits come back; they don't want to see us in that dark place. They need to demonstrate that they are not in hell or purgatory. On the contrary, from their perspective it is we who are held in a very dark place, as I don't think there's any Spirit dimension that is heavier than this one. It's hell when you go through the loss of a loved one and believe them gone forever – and nothing can be worse than that.

I've encountered many people who believe that breaching

the vale and contacting the Spirit world is a dangerous thing to do, and that Spirits will somehow grasp that opportunity to come back and possess or attack us. I've yet to see any episodes of this, and, as I said, the Spirits undergo a revelation on passing over that lifts them and frees them from human evils. I've never yet met a so-called 'evil Spirit' or been affected by one, despite being open to them every time I tune into the other world. They are purely benevolent beings and it's impossible to imagine them rounding on the living. Once more, it's people on earth who torment themselves.

If a Spirit was a malevolent person in life, he or she will need our prayers in order to progress in the Spirit life, and they are incapable of harming us any more – their struggle is with their own conscience instead. If we tell ourselves that something evil is holding us back, we will be held back – by ourselves, not the troubled Spirit. If we send compassion and prayers to them, we will move on, as will they.

I was on a tour of America with the wonderful medium Sylvia Browne when a member of the audience told her that she thought she was possessed by the devil. Sylvia delivered some Bronx compassion sharpish – 'Who are you to be possessed by Satan? Why you? Why not the Pope or somebody that'd get attention? Anyway, you can't be because I married the devil and his name's Vinnie and he's from Chicago.' No nonsense for

Sylvia! It was true – well, maybe apart from the bit about her ex-husband – and I bet that lady started feeling better in no time. Or else she'd have had Sylvia to answer to!

Another misconception shared by lots of people I have spoken to is the conviction that they themselves are somehow holding back their loved ones in Spirit. Because they haven't overcome their grief and miss them so dreadfully, the Spirit feels dragged down. 'Of course you're not holding him back,' I always assure them, as I know from many messages from the other side that the journey the Spirits are on is progressive and one-way.

They may choose to try to help us, but nothing that we do can hold them back. Even if they give us many messages over a period of years, they are still progressing. All that happens when we think we're clinging to them is that we are in fact stopping ourselves working through the natural stages of bereavement and are adding guilt to our troubles.

When I first became interested in using my mediumistic skills I attended a development class at a local Spiritualist church and spent many years building my skills up. I was still working as a hairdresser full-time in a city barber's in Glasgow. One night the boss and I were working late when a woman of forty or so came in. She looked awful – exhausted and bedraggled, and carrying a dozen bags – and we got her sat down as quickly as we could. She asked if she could just have her hair washed and I said I'd certainly do it.

As I started she was completely silent. It was a very profound silence too, as though she had no energy even to think, and I found it weighing on me. In the end I had to ask if she was ok, and something ran right through her body as she sighed. When you're a hairdresser people tell you things they wouldn't dream of telling anyone else – especially if they see you as a stranger they'll never have to see again – and I had the feeling she really needed someone to confide in. She seemed ready to burst. Whatever had happened to her must have been all but unbearable.

She said, 'I'm having the most terrible, terrible time, son. I'm moving house.' I did my hairdresser thing and sympathized as I rinsed her hair out, saying, 'Oh, isn't that the most stressful thing you can do? Is it a nice house you're moving to?' Then she began at the beginning, and told me the whole story.

Her husband had died of a heart attack when he was only in his early middle age. I nodded, but was suddenly aware of a Spirit gentleman being present. He gave me his name, and showed me himself standing by a taxi, for some reason. I was about to tell the lady but I bit my tongue and thought better. I decided to listen to more of her tale.

She'd gone to a Spiritualist church and got a message from

him that had left her overjoyed and closer than ever to him. I began blow-drying her hair gently, still listening to her while the Spirit man poured out more evidence. It felt as though I had one ear on each of the couple! Something still stopped me explaining it to the wife as she sat before me in the chair, talking softly.

She went on to tell me that she'd been so happy that she'd told her son about the message, but he was furious. He belonged to a very extreme Christian movement and he was horrified by what she'd done. He let rip, shouting, 'How could you? How could you pull my father back when he's progressing?' He seized her and dragged her to a church meeting by the scruff of her neck and told everyone what she'd done.

They turned on her and denounced her, but she insisted that she knew that he was ok and that giving that message hadn't hurt him in the least. She'd felt so good when she got the communication that she couldn't and wouldn't be persuaded that it hadn't been the right thing to do. When the Christian group heard this they became convinced that she had been attacked and taken over by something wicked and began to beat her viciously, trying physically to drive the 'demon' out, cursing her for bringing that evil into their church.

The minister himself had punched her in the solar plexus, I remember her telling me in a trembling voice. She was hurt so badly that she'd ended up bruised and vomiting. She couldn't stay with her son after that and had run away. She didn't even dare think of her husband any more – she was terrified that the people at the church were right, and she had done him harm.

She told me her husband's name – it matched the one the Spirit gentleman had given me – and that he had been a taxi driver. By this point I knew why I'd felt I shouldn't pass on the messages he was giving me. I'm sure that if this random hairdresser had started telling her about her husband on the Spirit side she would be so scared that she would have thought it was just as the church had told her – that Satan was throwing things in her path.

So I carried on brushing her hair and asked her, 'If you loved your husband, do you really think you could hold him back? Because I don't really know anything about this stuff, but I don't think you could.' And she said, 'Well, that's true.' She said he'd been her best friend as well as her lover; they'd had a very, very close bond. 'So,' I said, 'don't you think he'd *want* to come through?'

'Well, yes.'

'Do you feel you want to talk to him? Because you know what, if I'd lost someone I'd want to talk to them.'

'I'm dying to talk to him but I'd be holding him back.'

'Do you think you could hurt him when you loved him so much? I don't think so. And anything that's as extreme as that church and says you can't contact someone you love, whether they're dead or alive, can't be any good.' I was warming to my theme, as what she needed from the Spirit world wasn't words but some sanity. Just by being able to talk and get some common sense back, she was relaxing visibly.

As I was putting the finishing touches to her hair she said, 'You're right. It can't be wrong, what I did. And I knew that.'

'The message you got in the spooky place,' I said, meaning the Spiritualist church – I didn't want to give anything away – 'How did you feel?'

She turned in her chair and looked at me and said, 'I felt warm. I felt alive for the first time since his death. I felt a reconnection, I felt *strong* again.'

I put a hand on her shoulder and said, 'Can I just say something to you? I think you should just go with your feelings. I don't think you need to rush back to that Spiritualist place. If that felt ok, I don't think it's wrong of you to think of your husband because you'd never hold him back. How could you?' It was as though I was giving her permission, and that was the message that came directly from her husband.

Before she left I asked if she had a picture and she fished one out of one of her bags showing him standing in front of his taxi and I knew for sure he'd definitely been there as I was washing her hair.

She'd missed her husband, pure and simple, but it's seldom

true that the relationship between the one who has passed and the one who is left behind is so uncomplicated, as people rarely die what you might call 'tidy deaths', having set all their affairs in order. There is almost always a mass of unfinished emotional business that people are at a loss to sort out and this can contort the process of grieving in all kinds of ways. It can be difficult to distinguish between the actual sense of shock and loss and the other emotions that crowd in, and the mourner misinterprets all these and finds themselves lost in a maze of destructive feelings. Most commonly, people are angry with the person who has passed for any one of a number of reasons, and they feel ashamed because they are thinking ill of the dead, so *then* they become guilty too.

Memories that have been repressed or forgotten resurface as we think over the life that has just ended, and they all have to be dealt with in turn before the death of our loved one can be accepted. A sitting with a medium can help to tie up these loose ends, as it were, but it still takes a lot of work from the bereaved to accept what those in the Spirit world have to tell them.

Spirits exist in a higher state of emotional awareness and that's why they seem much wiser than they were in their time in this life. They have lost the restraints and other fears that stopped them understanding these things and have clarity of mind that can be enlightening for those they have left behind. They can give information which their loved one on earth never dreamed they knew about them, and it is done with the aim of helping them to move on and stop being wracked by other negative emotions like anger and guilt.

I once gave a sitting to a widow who had had suffered from depression all her life, but never discussed it with her husband of thirty years. She'd thought he just had no interest in her happiness, and now that he was gone she didn't know if she should mourn him or resent what she saw as years of neglect. He came through to tell her that he had known all along that she was troubled, but that he had been scared to face it, so had just never let her know how acutely he felt her distress.

His own mother had had a nervous breakdown when he was young and he had been so hurt by that that he had gone into denial when he realized his own wife was ill. This explanation cast their relationship in a whole new light and his widow was able to understand a side of her husband that she had never thought existed.

Of course, the knowledge that the life you have lost is not actually over can also cause guilt. If our loved ones in Spirit have this new insight, what do they know about things we might have tried to conceal from them in life? Many people find that death is a great teacher, and they have to take stock of their own behaviour when a loved one passes. The lesson is learned late, but is still valid, and it can go a long way to bringing 'closure' if you can take it to heart.

A man was once referred to me who seemed to be in a bad way; his body language was agitated in the extreme, and before I could even begin he told me that he had come to see a medium because he had had several affairs during his marriage and now that his wife had passed, he had had an awful dawning realisation that perhaps she knew exactly what he'd got up to behind her back. Now of course, he was filled with remorse and wished he could have confessed it to her when she was still alive.

When I tuned into Spirit, his wife made contact and traded the usual pieces of proof so that he would know she was in touch from the Spirit side. He accepted all this, but I could see that he was still waiting for some kind of bombshell as he fidgeted in his chair. Throughout the half-hour sitting his wife never mentioned that he had cheated on her, but just offered him memory after memory of their time together.

There was no sense of resentment coming through from her, but only the reiteration that she loved him and wished he would stop torturing himself. I don't know how you could tell if she knew about his infidelities or not; she certainly chose not to mention them directly. By focusing him on the better times in their marriage she may have been hinting indirectly that she did, but she was also pushing back the heavy guilt that was consuming his mind to make room for more positive feelings.

CHAPTER THREE

Truth Hurts

Truth Hurts

There are people who back away from even the first steps of coming to terms with death. It might seem bizarre that someone might go into a form of denial and pretend that they are unaffected or even that the death hasn't happened at all, but I've seen it happen plenty of times.

Ignoring your grief in this way takes a constant effort which is every bit as exhausting as trying to keep yourself immersed in deep depression. Eventually you will be so mentally exhausted that you will not have the mental reserves to cope with the reality of your situation when it inevitably breaks through to you.

At a book signing a couple of years ago I was answering questions when a woman who must have been somewhere in her fifties completely floored me. 'My mother has just passed, but do you think that she can actually be dead if I don't believe it?' I didn't know what to make of this, so I asked her what she meant. Did she mean she was still alive spiritually, because that was certainly the case.

'No,' said the lady. 'I mean physically. If I keep doing the things I used to do for her and pick up the phone to call her and lay out her clothes for her, won't she still be with me?'

I don't think she was quite thinking of a Norman Bates-style arrangement with her poor deceased mum propped up at the dining-room table, but she wasn't exactly handling things well either. I told her the only thing I could, that she must accept her mother's death and realize that she was no longer in the physical world, but she cut in and told me that she *had* to keep doing these things as it stopped her feeling sad.

I hope she had someone close to her, a friend or a family member who could step in so that she wasn't alone with these delusions. She needed someone to be honest with her and to support her when she faced her grief, and it didn't look like I was the person to talk her out of her fantasy.

I've known people go to elaborate lengths to reason that really they're ok, and they are coping with everything just fine. I think the most haunting case I came across was that of a young woman who attended my Spiritualist church. She let us know that she had lost a very young child – a little girl – in tragic circumstances, and I understood that she'd had a string of other personal problems which came to a head in the wake of the baby's death.

Mrs Primrose, who was a medium and teacher at the church, said we should perform a healing for the woman, who was called

Pat, but Pat insisted that she didn't need a healing as she had done her grieving while her daughter was terminally ill. She had, she insisted, accepted her loss and she was only going to the church so that she could help others in similar circumstances.

Mrs Primrose confided to me that she thought the woman didn't realize she'd suffered a loss, but I couldn't agree. She seemed very together, always making incisive comments and being ready to talk to other people about their difficulties. Mrs P told me I was wrong. It was only a short time since the baby had passed, and she couldn't believe that Pat wasn't burying her real feelings.

She'd been a regular at the church for a while when one evening, during an open demonstration of mediumship, the visiting medium on the platform singled Pat out and said that she had a little girl in the Spirit world. Her reaction was explosive. 'Don't you dare!' she spat. 'You have no business giving me a message. I *dealt* with that. Don't you bring my daughter back to me.' She ran out, tears streaming down her face.

We thought it was best to leave her for a while, and she reappeared at the end of the demonstration when everyone was milling around. She looked very composed and just said, 'You know what that was about? I had a miscarriage and that's what that message was about. Not my daughter. She's fine in the Spirit world and I told her not to come back to me and it's all fine.'

After this, she seemed to go downhill rapidly. Mrs Primrose kept an anxious eye on her, but she refused all help, adamant that she was there to help others and she herself was ok. She lost a lot of weight and her behaviour got increasingly erratic. One day when I was working at the barber's she walked in the door and came straight up to me. I was cutting someone's hair at the time, and was surprised to see her.

She said something very odd. 'Why have you not brought my daughter to me?'

When I said I had no idea what she was talking about she repeated, 'Why have you not brought my daughter to me?', her voice rising to a hysterical edge.

I told her I wouldn't talk to her till she had calmed herself a bit and she sat down and started to tell me, as though I knew exactly what she was on about, that I had started to appear to her through other people. I told her I'd never done such a thing.

'Don't fool with me,' she said with a steely tone. 'You're the one person who hasn't tried to give me a message and I know you're the one who's got it.'

I swore I had no idea what she was talking about, trying to be as quiet and as firm as I could. She seemed to take this on board and left the shop, leaving me fearful for her mental state. Later the same day she came back, with a fresh determination. Slowly she began her explanation. I was, she said, materialising in her house and giving her a message about her daughter but she couldn't understand it because I was projecting myself in an astral state and she wasn't in an astral state and so it wasn't coming out right.

I shook my head, seriously concerned and wondering how to get through to her. 'I don't have that message and I can't astrally project myself about the place.'

'Yes, you can.' She was full of conviction, and nothing I said was going to shake her off. 'And there are Spirit people there too and they want me to cross over and be with my daughter.'

'Have you been to your doctor? You've got so thin. Don't you think you should see a doctor and tell him about all the things you've got on your mind? You don't need me, love, you need your GP.' Her eyes were hollow, and I could only imagine when she last slept. Mrs Primrose had been right, and now Pat had clearly moved on into a new reality and she wanted a medium to validate that reality, by telling her that the 'Spirits' she'd been seeing were the genuine article.

She was furious, screaming that I was patronising her, and that I was trying to keep her away – that we were all trying to keep her away – from her daughter. Then she raced outside and began attacking my car. She must have brought something with her to do it – who knew why? – and now she was laying into the bonnet and windscreen, smashing the headlights, scratching away frantically at the sides. Eventually her anger and her energy seemed to ebb and she left, leaving me to contemplate my mangled car and rack my brains to think what the hell I could do to help her. I certainly could not give her a reading. The last thing she needed was contact with a Spirit world she couldn't physically touch or sense – she must be grounded, and be able to trust her own perception once more. She also needed to be with good friends who would talk to her about her daughter's death and let her start to accept it.

When I phoned Mrs Primrose she said she'd been worried something like this would happen. She'd seen Pat keeping a vigil outside her house at nights, waiting for some kind of sign. When Mrs P had gone out to talk to her, Pat had hurried away into the dark. No wonder she looked so exhausted.

Someone did get through to Pat eventually, a good friend who coaxed her to a doctor who recognized how ill she was and got her started on a course of treatment immediately. She did recover, and also made it back to work after some time off, but she never came back to the Spiritualist church, which I think was wise. I heard from her friend that Pat had been surrounded by friends and colleagues who had been uncomfortable dealing with her when she was in shock at her daughter's illness and death, and hadn't offered her much other than tosh about lights at the end of the tunnel and time being a great healer. As Pat got sick she had persuaded herself that she could talk to her daughter, and became torn between wanting a message from the Spirit world and the knowledge that if one came through, it would mean that her child was dead. She'd pretended to herself and everyone else that she was over her mourning while secretly thinking her baby had never passed over.

You cannot fight your grief. Denying it its expression will only work in the short term, and then you may well find yourself in a very bad place indeed.

From one extreme to, I suppose, another. If there are people who try to forget about their bereavement, there are also those who try to build their loss into something it's not. It's less dangerous, but very silly and tactless, to over-dramatize our relationship to someone who has passed over just for the sake of grieving extravagantly and drawing attention to ourselves.

I'll always remember being at a friend's mother's funeral and standing at the graveside with her and her siblings as the body was being committed to the earth. All at once a cousin of theirs pushed through the gathered mourners and started screaming that she could not, just could not, go on without her aunt. People took her hands and soothed her as she sobbed, pulling her away from the grave as she looked like she was about to fling herself into it. She carried on whimpering noisily throughout the committal.

My friend caught my eye and I saw she looked absolutely disgusted. She and her brothers had lost their mother, but they were trying to make it through her funeral with dignity, to give tribute to her. As the funeral party broke up and moved off, the cousin fixed on me and hung off my arm, telling me I must help her contact her aunt or else she'd die herself. I patted her shoulder and gave her a few pointless platitudes.

There was no way I was tuning into the Spirit world at a time like that, when the deceased's immediate family were raw with grief. I had known my friend's mother well too, and I was pretty sure she wouldn't want to talk to this cousin after that display. Later my friend told me that the cousin hadn't been in touch with her mother for twenty years or more and in her younger days had been known to pull all sorts of elaborate tricks just to get attention.

You should never grieve more than your mind allows you to. There is nothing positive about turning your memory of your connection with the deceased into something it wasn't. It's another form of denial, and an insult to the person who has passed, as it's a false version of what they really were to you. Loss stings us to the core, and when we look at the loss of someone we loved, the most honest way of dealing with it is to measure your feelings against your memory. Your pain will be proportionate to your bond to that person in life.

I have seen so many people run from their grief and change it into something else, finding it easier to fight or argue with the living, as the dead seem to have gone into a realm of the untouchables. Many people, in their unfinished argument with the people they have lost, turn their anger on those around them.

Some refuse to move out of the grieving state, because they feel that ever to be happy again will be the greatest betrayal to the one they lost. People who become stagnant in their grief are so hard to reach, as they make a personal war against life and all who are living in it. God forbid that anyone should ever be happy around them, as, if they are in mournful pain, then everyone should be.

It is when I meet someone like this that I feel that a message from their loved one is never enough; they have switched themselves off from all communication and no matter what you offer, they will be very hard to shift from the grief which has become cemented around them. It is a very difficult position to be in, when all you wish to do is help and you are not equipped with answers or the ability to bring their loved one back. Sometimes a breakthrough can be made, though, but the mourner must be willing to learn the lesson they are being offered.

A fellow medium once told me a story about a man who had turned up at her local Spiritualist church when there was no service on and, having found the caretaker, told him that he must have a sitting with my friend or else he would kill himself. He'd lost his wife some years earlier to multiple sclerosis. They'd been hugely successful partners in business as well as life and had no children; they'd been about to embark on a well-deserved retirement together when she was diagnosed.

The husband had spent masses of money on private health-care and they tried all sorts of alternative treatments but it couldn't stem the course of the disease. As a businessman he'd been used to being able to overcome any problems they faced by making some canny decision or another, but he was powerless to stop his wife's decline. She was very stoical, which almost made things worse because he couldn't even be the strong one for her – she was doing that for herself. Nurses and doctors moved in and took over the care work, leaving him on the sidelines, unable to make a difference in the only way he knew how.

When she passed he was inconsolable. He tried to throw money at the problem once again, seeing expensive private counsellors or therapists, but he dismissed their efforts as worthless. Nobody, he said, could understand what he was going through, and there would be no relief but death. He told friends he wanted to kill himself, and they, alarmed, sent him to a Spiritualist church, but he didn't like the medium there and recommenced his suicide threats.

He seemed determined to put himself beyond help, and

those around him were terrified that having lost his wife, they were now losing him – he was barely the person they'd known before – and would lose him once and for all if he carried out his promise. He didn't give up on his quest to find the right medium, though, hence he'd tracked down my friend and insisted on the private sitting. She heard on the grapevine from his friends too, who were at their wits' end, that his case was a grave one.

The upshot was that at the sitting this man's wife came through and gave him the rollicking of his life. She'd known very well that it was her attention he'd been trying to get by acting that way, and she didn't want to see him put himself or their friends through this selfish behaviour. She was, she told my friend who told the husband, disgusted by what he was doing.

This blast from the other side was all the confirmation her husband needed – she was still with him, and she was still most emphatically the no-nonsense woman he'd loved in life. He started laughing and didn't stop for the rest of the sitting, delighted to have his wife back. My friend was astonished at the change in him, as in seconds he seemed to warm back into the generous, affable man he'd once been and he left the session with a promise to her and his wife in Spirit that he would mend his ways.

Grief is a pain which we experience on our own – it is individual to each person and dealt with separately according to each on his or her own. In a family situation when many people mourn the same loss, this can cause all kinds of different dynamics that affect everyone. Sometimes it binds people together more strongly, or makes links where there were only tentative or troubled relationships before. Sometimes, though, a death can blow a family apart altogether.

It is one of the reasons why, as a medium, I like to see people separately if I can, as often the Spirit whom they wish to communicate with meant different things to different people with whom they were connected. And there are times when it would seem that one person gets more out of a sitting with a medium, leaving others feeling unappreciated.

I've seen this played out when families come to see me for a private sitting. Maybe a son who has died has directed more of the information to the mother or father or sibling, which is felt acutely by the others who are left out. I have heard families having quarrels at the end of their sitting about why the deceased should mention only so-and-so's gift to them last year and not theirs, or have such a special message for his sister but not his father. It's the worst kind of squabbling, pitting people who are all in deep grief against one another, and no good can come of it.

It is difficult enough for the Spirit to make their information clear to me, without having to dot all the i's and cross all the t's for everyone. Most people accept when I explain to them that the time we have is limited and that with the best will in the world I cannot describe a person's life, memories and connections to their entire family in the space of a half hour or one hour. Yet I have become aware that when a whole family loses one of its close members, unless they become strong and help one another as a unit, there is every chance that they will implode. I'm sure that the Spirit people would not wish to see the people they love destroyed like this because of their death.

Two sisters I knew from Aberdeen didn't speak a word to each other for months after their father's death, as each considered themselves in more pain and worse affected than the other. Each claimed to have been closer to their father and also to have done more for him, and spoke openly about this to the rest of their family and friends. It was the younger of the two that came to me for a sitting, some six months after her father's death. During the sitting her father gave vent to his disappointment at the behaviour of two people he loved and told his daughter that she must take the recording of the sitting back to her sister and let her hear the message, which mentioned that he would not be happy until both his girls realized that they were being childish and hurtful to one another. He also stated that he knew how both of them loved him and he wanted them to love each other as they loved him and he would be happy.

I got the sense that this man had had to give his daughters a telling off many times before as they both competed for his attention during his life and here they were again on his death, each wanting his favour more than the other. Recently I spoke to his younger daughter who tells me that she took the cassette recording home to her sister and they listened together. They took his words to heart this time and are getting on very well, reminiscing about their father and sharing him with each other.

In cases like this, each person wants the other to know that they feel pain and each will display it differently, but what they really want to do is to help one another, hold one another and tell each other that everything will be ok. Sometimes a show of strength or acceptance at the death of a loved one is interpreted by others as a betrayal. They might think that if there is no outward showing of grief you didn't really care, or you have gotten over it too quickly and are unfeeling.

I was asked by an acquaintance if I would give a private sitting to a family who, unbeknownst to me, had lost their daughter in early 2001. She had died along with several other teenage friends in a house fire, and left a mother and father, both in their fifties, two brothers who were in their twenties and a sister of maybe thirty. I met them at their home in a very beautiful part of England later that same year.

We were all seated in the living room when I began to ask in my head if anyone in the Spirit world wanted to communicate.

No sooner had the thought gone out when I received a picture of a pretty and plump young woman with short blonde hair whom I described to them. Then I heard a voice which I felt came from her and she mentioned a fire and at this news everyone in the room with me began to weep.

During the sitting the young woman managed to get enough information through to convince them that she was really communicating with them and added important things to try to bring some comfort to them. She wasn't suffering, she assured them, and she had blacked out and felt no pain at the time of her death. She gave different little bits of evidence to some of them, but not everyone was given a special message from her. All in all, however, the sitting appeared to have been a success and the family looked uplifted. There was a buzz about them which had not been there at the start.

A week later the father phoned me and asked if he could have a second sitting on his own and if I would give another sitting to his youngest son who hadn't had a personal message the first time. He said he had felt let down by his sister in the Spirit world.

I said I couldn't, imagining how this situation would spiral out of control, with me giving sitting after sitting to try and 'even up' the communication. The father told me he was going to separate from his wife and move into a new house with his youngest son, as neither his wife nor their other children could understand what they were going through. His daughter, he insisted to me, had meant more to him and his youngest son than to any of the others. He pleaded with me, saying he still had issues to clear up with his Spirit daughter that hadn't been mentioned at the sitting.

I still refused to see the man as I felt a strong sensation in my stomach which I always get when the Spirits are telling me that I shouldn't do something. I was polite to this man and tried to answer his questions the best I could, but all the time I just wanted to remind him that all of his family had suffered a loss when his daughter went over. Instead, I listened and let him go over and over how no-one but he felt the enormity of grief and that his daughter should know what he was feeling.

Eventually I did get through to him that of course she knew exactly what he was going through, as this is where the Spirit people reach us – in our thoughts and through our feelings – but he was having none of it. He would not accept that anyone was hurting like he and his son, and he reiterated that he had to make his daughter aware of this. It becomes difficult to explain to someone in this state that you don't need a medium to tell your loved ones in the Spirit world what you feel and think. Those on the other side will pick up on this and that's why they try to let you know they are still in touch with you. I don't know what happened to that family in the end, and I can only hope they realized how destructive they had been to one another.

After this episode, I began to see how families can use grief as a weapon on one another, and how selfish people can become because they have suffered a loss. I remember my own aunt and uncle separated for a year following the death of their only son, after constantly arguing over who was hurting more and who had been more affected by his passing. The year they had apart taught them that they needed each other, as no-one else around them could empathize with the pain that each of them was feeling. No-one else had known and loved their son so well either.

When they got back together they handled the grief as a partnership and assisted one another. I think that as a family you have to be strong and understanding with each other, aware of the pain which you are all experiencing and learn that each one has their own methods of coping.

Where family or group grief is concerned, I do feel that openness about feelings is important, but remember that each part of that group is where you are, have been, or will be. Different members of the family will be at varying stages in the grieving process; also, the emotional states of different individuals will vary at the time of someone's death. It can be difficult to think of all these factors and be understanding when you are in the grip of depression yourself, but doing so pays greater dividends by far than shutting out your nearest and dearest.

Those outside the immediate circle of the bereaved can be invaluable in seeing someone through grief, playing as practical or as emotionally supportive a role as the nature of their friendship allows. It is true though that at some point, no matter how well- meaning or kind a person is, they will pull back their attention and aid if they do not see a change in the bereaved in response to the good energy they have given out. This is generally the point at which the person who has lost a loved one needs to make an effort for themselves to become better.

If they hold onto their pain in order to get attention from others – perhaps to try to compensate for what they lost when their loved one passed – the people around them become exhausted and avoid them rather than be pulled into the vacuum created from self- pity and emotional need. As no-one can ever hope to replace the deceased, that vacuum will go unresolved.

I recall a woman who was a friend of one of the hairdressers I worked with, who had lost her partner of twenty-odd years. She would often call the salon to speak to my colleague in the middle of the working day, or turn up unannounced to cry on her shoulder, never recognising that my friend was busy with a client. She constantly asked me if I could see her partner or get any message from him as she was so desperately sad.

At first I did try to give the lady a sitting and even got a link with her partner, but I found that she was not satisfied. She said she still felt bad and that what I had told her wasn't enough. She wanted more from him. After two years of this sort of behaviour my colleague was exasperated and her friend kept telling her that no-one else would listen to her and she missed her partner so much she wanted to give up on life itself.

My friend stopped taking her phone calls as she'd exhausted every shred of comfort she could offer the woman. The final straw had come during one of her long outpourings on the telephone, when my colleague gently tried to bring her friend up short and tell her she was at work, with a client with half a haircut whom she had to attend to, and the other woman retorted that obviously the hairdresser's work came before their precious friendship, and slammed the phone down.

This type of behaviour is disgraceful and ill-mannered, whatever the circumstances, and made my colleague feel very bad when she was on the receiving end. Bereavement is not an excuse to behave like a spoiled child and will only drive away those who can help you. I also felt that no message from the other side would have helped this woman while she was in such a state of self-pity, as it is one of the most materially heavy, self-imposed conditions the mind can create and is the opposite of the spiritual thinking which can allow your loved one in Spirit to get close to you.

CHAPTER FOUR

Realising Life Beyond Death

Realising Life Beyond Death

When I was taking part in a Spiritualist development group in Glasgow at the end of the 1980s I had an experience that I wrote about in my first book, *Spirit Messenger*, but at the time I used the story to illustrate how trance mediumship worked. Now I realize that the message taught me instead that we often fear our life more than our death.

We'd reached the end of a group meditation session when one of the mediums, Laura, went into a trance, a method which allows the mind of a Spirit to communicate with the living using her body. This time, a man's voice spoke through her as she sat motionless, eyes closed, only her mouth moving. The man didn't seem to be at ease or euphoric in the way that Spirits usually appear to be; in fact he sounded scared.

He told us that he was 'stuck' and afraid. We began to ask him questions and he gave us his name, and said that he was in one of the big Glasgow hospitals and that his body was dying. He said that he was afraid to die because he was sure he was going to be punished for things he had done in his life. He spoke fluently, describing the scene at his bedside, where his wife and three daughters were sitting vigil over him in his coma.

They were all crying for him, and he didn't want to leave them so distressed. He also understood that they could not and must not be kept in that state of awful suspended grief. He needed to let go and end their agony, but he was petrified about what lay ahead.

I can still remember how Mrs Primrose took over and talked to the voice of the man as though he was physically there in the room with us and there was nothing strange about the whole scene. She told him he had to look at those bad memories which he could feel pushing to the front of his mind and face up to them. When he was ready, she said, there would be a light which he could follow and he would find his fear lifting away. He'd be able to let go and release his family.

After a short pause there was a sense that Laura was breathing more deeply, and she began to move again and to open her eyes. She related her own experience, which had included a vision of the man's wife and daughters in the hospital room. We subsequently found out by phoning the hospital that a man of the same name had indeed been a patient in one of their wards. A few days later someone from the development group phoned to tell me that they had seen his obituary in the local newspaper, saying that he had passed peacefully in hospital and would be missed by his wife and three daughters.

Now, I'm sure you're familiar with the idea that when you are passing over, you feel as though you are moving toward a bright light, but what I think is more interesting in this story is the way that the dying man found his life story running back through his mind. Many of the Spirits that I have communicated with have confirmed this to me, that their death itself is exhilarating, and that as they pass, their being is immediately focused on the life they have just left on earth.

The important emotional episodes which they shared with those they have been separated from become more and more vivid and essential and are animated from mere memories to a full-blown experience which they can relive. I suppose this is a bit like waking up the morning after and going back over what you got up to the night before – but a million times more so! It's a lifetime's worth of recollections, good and bad.

In re-experiencing their memories they undergo some kind of enlightenment and healing which cause them to understand the purpose of their earthly existence, however short or long a span it lasted. They come to terms with their life and all that happened in it, and recognize reasons for all the things in their life. Everything that happened to them was a lesson that enabled them to experience different emotions and no matter what occurred while they were on this path, they have arrived pretty much where they should have.

This 'eureka' moment is palpable to me as a medium, and when I give a sitting to their loved ones some of that energy transfers to them too, leaving them empowered and in a much lighter state of mind than when they first arrived. In their new reality the Spirits are filled with hope and understanding which come from a sense of freedom from suffering and despair. They perceive a tremendous broadening of their mental capacity for life, living and growing.

They may realize things about their lives with their loved ones that give them a startling new perspective. This is what leads some Spirits to try to contact those they have left behind, in order to explain themselves. They are in touch also because they want us to know that they still exist and we can still bridge the gap their physical death brought about. They give us a glimpse of their new existence and enough evidence to convince us so that we too can know we are Spirit and part of a greater consciousness, and will, like them, grow and expand when we are freed from our physical body. This is the deepest meaning that we can read from their visits and the best response we can have is to acknowledge their presence and think of them in a positive way.

As I made clear earlier, the Spirits are freed of the human drives which cause such misery on this earth – the needs to possess or to control other things and people. This is the beginning of what I've talked about as 'progression' in the afterlife. Some people arrive at a considerable understanding of Spirit before their deaths, and they will inevitably progress more easily. That doesn't mean that those who were troubled in their lifetime won't advance in Spirit, however. With their new insight they will overcome these problems and resolve them.

I spoke to a lady at a seminar I took part in who told me she'd seen a medium shortly after her husband died and said that she was given superb evidence that his Spirit had survived. This message had helped her cope with his death and her own mixed emotions. She'd subsequently attended a Spiritualist service and had a further communication via another medium and this time her husband had told her that he had now learned to overcome his anger and apologized for all the times that he had lost his temper with her and their children.

The interesting thing is that though she told me she'd loved and missed him very much, his aggression was the one thing that blighted her memory of their years together, and had made her in turn feel guilty as she grieved. We chatted about the afterlife and progression, as she was interested to know what her husband was going through now. I reassured her that he was not being punished by any being but himself. Every individual must deal with their own conscience, embracing that expansion that is possible on acceptance of this responsibility. If they turn away from it, their conscience will grow heavy and stagnant.

He was learning from his life and refining his conscience in a more spiritual way by accepting responsibility for both good and bad things that he had done, having chosen expansion. In Spirit, he would see not only the immediate effect of his actions on earth, but also the more far-reaching consequences. Let me try to explain a little how this works.

If you were rude to someone for no reason at all, but pretended not to be bothered by what you'd done, you could be sure that eventually your conscience would pull you up. If you were a fair-minded person you'd then learn from that and try not to do it again. In Spirit you would see not only how you'd hurt that person, but also how they might have taken their own anger out on someone else, and so on in a chain reaction. You'd see how it all began with your spite, and that your conscience would bear the whole weight of that action.

One of the most moving sittings I ever gave concerned a Spirit who had undergone this process and who was able to change the lives of his loved ones as a result. I was giving a series of private sittings in Germany a couple of years ago, and during the afternoon readings, a mother and teenage son were ushered into the room.

I'll never forget the contrast between the two of them.

The woman must have been about forty but she looked like she'd been put through a wringer, as though she'd been crying for years at a time. The boy was excited, hopeful. I learned later that they had come all the way from Austria for the reading and that they were so poor that the son had had to insist that his mother spent money for his Christmas presents on the train fare.

Even without knowing that I felt a desperate urge to help them; I was trying so hard when I started to tune myself in that at first I got nothing back. After a few minutes a man came through who turned out to be the father of the family, and I had a sense of something apologetic, almost humble, reaching out to them. He showed me himself on a motorcycle, and when I told his wife she sat up and looked really interested.

I asked her if her husband had had a tattoo of an eagle on his left arm, and she nodded. I said he'd shown me that he was now as free as an eagle. She laughed and I asked her if she had a matching tattoo, and she pulled up her sleeve to show it to me. When they were young and in love they'd been bikers, and those had been the best times they'd shared together.

The man went on to say that it wasn't her fault but his. As the sitting went on I discovered that he'd become an abusive and possessive husband who hadn't even let his wife go out to work as he was so jealous. Their son had loved his father, but had had to cope with seeing him turn on his mother. The father said he was especially ashamed about that.

He knew in Spirit that his son was doing brilliantly at school, and when he conveyed that to the son he said a tremendous thing: 'If I was still in your life you could not have done so well. I love you, but I could never have shown you that.' He'd been miserable and horrible to his son and wife, the two people who had loved him most in the world. He'd made their lives hell, and now he was able to understand just what he'd inflicted on them.

The boy's reaction was like a dam-burst. He was so relieved to have this release; I can only imagine how he'd suffered watching his mother sink into depression, and how she had become even worse after his father's death. I think that both of them had been relieved when the man passed, but this made them feel guilty. Now he had come back to give them permission to cast that off, and I could see them being transformed as it dawned on them both.

To his wife he said that she deserved a life and that she'd had no sort of existence with him there. As long as he was with them he would only have dragged them down, and now he was happy. He had also, in a strange twist, made it possible for them to love him as they never could have in life – an extraordinary gift.

When the session was over and the two of them left I actually broke down in tears myself. The change in the woman's whole being had been more astonishing than any I'd ever seen in two decades work as a medium. I hoped I'd be able to find out if they did in fact pick up the pieces of their lives and really flourish after that 'blessing' from the man who had ruined so much when he was alive.

I did see them again, a year later at another seminar. They were delighted to see me and filled me in on what had happened since. The woman looked great, as though she was ten years younger. She had gone back to her old job, and said she'd never felt so good. She told me she thought about her husband in his best light, remembering when they were young. 'I've let my memory go back there, and that is where I see him. I can see the goodness of the man – the other things that happened were from somewhere else.'

Her son was thriving too, achieving great grades at school. He was grateful to see his mother was free, and seemed to have put the awful things that happened in his childhood firmly behind him. I still think of the two of them and send them thoughts, and I know they do the same for the father.

Those who have committed serious crimes in their life must go through the same process of braving the evidence of their misdemeanours and seeing the consequences of them spiral out, devastating many people in their course. They will progress in the end, but it will take them much time and spiritual effort to do so.

I once gave a very odd message to a man, most of which I can't elaborate on in too much detail here. When I tuned into Spirit I felt nothing but darkness, which was very different to the sort of 'blank' sensation I get if there is no-one there for the sitter. Never before or since have I known such a heaviness of mind than when I linked to this Spirit being; I even felt physically sick, retching at times. The Spirit said that he was the man's father.

When I gave his name to the son he shouted out, 'No!' I've seldom seen someone so angry. He cried throughout the sitting with tears of pure fury. He'd wanted to get through to his mother to be sure that she wasn't with his father in Spirit, but it was the father himself who came through. Open as I was to the father's conscience, I began to see the things that he was having to face up to on the other side.

It turned out that he had killed one woman and raped several others. He showed me mentally that he had had to look at the victims themselves, and at their friends and families and what happened to them as they struggled to cope with what he had done. This knowledge was torturing him now, and he was trying to work his way through it alone.

In life he had been tried and imprisoned and his family had cut him out of their lives. He'd died when he was still serving his sentence. Now he asked for forgiveness from his son, to help him progress in Spirit. In order to go forward and expand, he was having to live through the pain he had created on earth and that would take him several lifetimes.

I can't write what the outcome of that sitting was, but something similar happened at another one-to-one reading that I gave, and the result of that one was a tremendous release. I was meeting a healer called Sandra. When I told her that I had her father there, she tensed up and said, 'I really don't want to listen to this message.' She looked scared and stony at the same time, as though she was gearing up to defend herself from a familiar enemy. I tried to go back to my guides and ask if there was anybody else there, but had a strong sense that her father's Spirit needed to get through.

Sandra was white-faced, watching me try, but I could see from her expression that she was wrestling with all kinds of thoughts. After a minute or two she tentatively said an incredibly brave thing: 'Give me the message. I think it's one I've needed to hear for a long time.' I didn't even ask her if she was sure, as I was getting the sense from both her and her father in Spirit that what was said would be incredibly important.

There was an implication in the message that Sandra had, as a child, suffered abuse at her own father's hands. In Spirit he was now begging for forgiveness. He had realized when he was still alive that what he had done was wrong, but hadn't been able to admit it to her. When he had died, nothing was resolved, and Sandra still despised him. He needed her to know what he had thought, and how painful it was for him to have turned that evil secret in on himself.

Now he talked to her about the years they had lost, saying, 'I've missed out because you've turned into a beautiful person, despite what I did to you.' He mentioned her work as a healer, and how she had turned her experience of what happened to her into a chance to help others, particularly children.

I can't say that Sandra was able then and there to sign off years of confusion and hatred and give him her blessing, but I believe his communication was the beginning of some kind of resolution for her. When the sitting was over we sat and hugged each other and she wept for a long time.

'I can't let him go because I've been swearing at him, cursing him and holding him back because he died and he never took responsibility for what he did. He died and we never got to talk about it.' She'd been stuck hating him, and now that was lifting away. He had also given her some kind of reason or excuse for what he'd done, which helped her. It was a strange, two-way healing, from the man in Spirit to his daughter in this life, and it took great spiritual courage for both of them to face up to it. I think both of them will be able to move on now.

When I talk about pain in the afterlife, I do not by any

stretch of the imagination mean physical pain. That belongs purely to this plane of existence. You should never labour under the delusion that your loved ones are still at the mercy of anything they suffered on earth. Sometimes the shock of a death in an accident, perhaps, or the slow agony of watching someone you care for deeply waste away from an illness grips the mind so much that when we think of the person who has passed we can only imagine them as terribly injured or wracked with pain.

When the Spirits try to persuade us that they are still in existence they want to drive home the point that they are beyond bodily suffering now, and that we should not think of them in that way. In the Spirit world they are whole once more. If we take this on board our own minds are freed to remember them in a positive light, and that will help us heal all the more swiftly.

It's hard not to write about the afterlife in a way that might give you the wrong idea – because it's such a different reality that it's difficult for us to comprehend in what little language we have. The Spirit can be in many places at the same time, and connect to many things simultaneously. That is why even if our loved ones do progress, they still keep their bond to us. They do not forget us.

Time does not really exist in Spirit as we experience it here. They are not aware of seconds or minutes or years, so it's never the case that a Spirit doesn't communicate in May because they are insufficiently advanced but they'll come through in October instead, when they've progressed a bit more. It is true that sometimes a message doesn't reach us because we are not ready to hear it, but that's a matter of time in our world, not Spirit.

Sometimes a communication can 'wait' as though it's on hold for the recipient either to be prepared for it or to be near a medium who can deliver it. It's also true that, as I explain in Chapter Six, that the Spirits have such a broad range of vision that they can see into our futures on this plane. When I was first exploring spiritualism my own family had an experience which shows both these phenomena.

I'd taken my mother and father to a Spiritualist demonstration because they were a bit worried about me at the time, and wanted to see what I was involving myself in. They'd never been to one before but went with open minds; as my father said: 'You look a lot happier, so whatever it is you're doing can't be bad.'

The medium who was working that night was Mrs Heskitt, who had come all the way from Wales and nobody in the church knew her. She was an excellent medium, and in no time the messages were coming through to people. After fifteen minutes or so she turned to my mother and said, 'Oh, my God, this is a message that has been waiting a long time. I have your mother here.'

My mum looked at me and hissed, 'What does she mean?' and I told her just to listen. My mother's mother died on Mum's wedding night in an accident, and my mum, who was nineteen at the time, had taken on the task of bringing up her four younger brothers and sisters. My father had become a second father to them too, as my granddad had long since left my grandmother.

Mrs Heskitt started to pass on the message to Mum. 'She's telling you that you've done a great job bringing up her family and that she's tried so hard all these years to try and help you but you're so stubborn you wouldn't let her. You have a job to do, and that's to get those children back safely to her once more, and when that's done you can reap the harvest of your life. You've sown all the seeds. Your mother will be waiting.'

Then she turned to my father and said, 'You've been a patient and tolerant man. I used to watch you cycle to work to feed my children. And you would cycle for miles. You did all this without my help.' The detail that she gave was remarkable, and all about things that had happened thirty or forty years ago. My grandmother had died in 1945, and Mrs Heskitt was standing there in front of us in 1985, finally passing on word from her.

The remarkable thing is that it is now twenty years since my parents got that word, and what my grandmother said came true. All my mother's younger siblings have died, one after the other in the last two years. My mother saw each of them gathered back to her own mother, just as she'd promised.

The other day I went to see her and she said, 'A funny thing happened. Maybe you'll understand it.' 'Oh yes,' I replied, wondering what on earth it could be. She told me that one of her great nephews had dreamt about *her* mother, who'd died long before he'd been born. We don't even have any pictures of her, so he would have had no idea what she looked like.

Kareem had said that in his dream his great-grandma had been surrounded by her four children who had passed over, and was saying, 'Tell Lizzie [my mother] she can stop worrying now.' I listened, and asked Mum, 'Do you take anything from that, mother?' And she said, 'I suppose I should stop worrying about them now, but how can you when you've worried about people all your life? It's what I do. It gives me something to do in that day time!'

The new reality that those who have passed over experience is totally different to our own. The Spirits know this, and often when they give evidence of their continued existence they put it in terms that we are likely to recognize. They have to give details of the sort of things they did in life, what they wore, how they looked, what music they listened to – any kind of stuff to get their message across. They may also convey the way in which they died.

If the people who are attending the sitting are still very afraid of death and the thought that their loved one has passed over, they need to have a more familiar and comforting version of the afterlife which is much more material in its appearance. Victorian Spiritualists built quite elaborate scenarios like this, describing Spirit homes and Spirit hospitals and universities – whole towns. They probably even had a Spirit barber or two!

These depictions of Spirits tend to show them as made of some kind of super-human flesh and blood, ageless and serene in their new world where nobody has any physical flaws. It's not what is going on at all, but it does create a sort of way of understanding, which enables those on earth to accept that their loved ones still exist.

Those who have a far greater understanding of the Spirit side tend to receive messages which don't bother with these kinds of bits of evidence, but are more ethereal and subtle and connected to emotions rather than physical concerns. The more you can shake off the idea that the dead are exactly as they were in human form, the more you will understand that your loved one is not progressing away from you, but instead being truly integrated into your life and your memory of them. This will help you grow spiritually yourself.

Imagine, if you can, what this world would be like if we couldn't hide our true feelings from one another, that everything you were thinking or feeling about someone else was known to them. In this world we are protected by our lack of sensitivity, and we bear grudges, feel negatively and hide our emotions. If we were to know what everyone was thinking all the time I'm sure we couldn't deal with them. We'd find ourselves living in chaos. As it is, we live in a darker world where there are shadows where we can hide and deny ourselves truth. Communication is limited to what we want others to hear and think of us and we have become so deluded ourselves that we can't remember what is reality and truth and what is our own artificial version.

In the Spirit world we cannot conceal our thoughts and emotions, and furthermore we just don't wish to. There are no masks or secrets. My friend Ros has been lucky to have several communications from her son, David, who passed to the other side some years ago. He has described the experience of meeting other Spirits in the afterlife as an interchange – Spirits expand on every contact with one another, taking on each other's knowledge. They allow each other to grow and uplift one another, reaching higher levels of what he calls 'luminosity'.

It's very difficult for us to understand it all in this life because I suppose we don't really have the words to describe it. Whatever we try to say about a Spirit existence will fall far short of what it will be like when we experience it ourselves. I imagine it would be like taking the greatest moment of your life – maybe the highest state of love you have ever been in, whether it be with a parent, partner, child or friend – and intensifying it a thousand times over.

The loss which we feel in the human side of death is like having that same experience taken away from us. In this grieving state people will fear that they will never be lifted to such states of happiness again, which causes them to feel empty and dark inside and totally disconnected from the love that they assume is gone forever. That bond doesn't have to be renewed via a medium or by going into a trance, but just by being open to Spirit, and letting your lost loved ones into your life.

I mentioned that many who are bereaved are crippled by a fear of death itself, a fear which I'm trying to explain is groundless. In the Western world today we don't seem to be prepared for mortality, and that makes grief unremittingly bleak. Many other cultures ease the way for both the dying and their loved ones, and by doing so help the one who has died to progress more rapidly and their family to handle their loss well.

I once watched a fascinating piece of video footage about a Tibetan family at the time of their father's death. A lama had been sent for to attend to him, and I was a bit shocked to see that he had seen fit to take a little boy along with him. I was told that the boy was a monk, and was learning how to perform the same procedure.

The lama then sent each member of the family in to see the dying man individually, to make their goodbyes. When they left he gave them each a 'practice' of prayers to do for the man out of his sight and hearing. He didn't want their weeping to hold the father back.

Once they were taken care of he encouraged the father to look for the highest place in the next life that he could, free from any emotional distraction. The boy repeated prayers with him and turned pages as he continued to guide the man. He told him that he was about to die, and that he should prepare himself for the next world. I was intrigued that each person in the family accepted the impending death absolutely and that nobody spooned out any platitudes to them or the dying man.

I saw true compassion and none of that watered-down guff that is so often doled out to those who are about to leave this world – that they'll be better in the morning, or that the situation will change. It was honest. If we all accepted our end in this world while still alive, the chances are that we would behave much better and more mindfully of others, knowing that it would affect our progress in the afterlife.

The fact that the lama gave the relatives a practice meant that by the time of the funeral – an air burial, when the body is left to the elements – their minds were already with the consciousness or Spirit of their father. They had maintained their bond and were helping him journey on.

Not all deaths enable the one who is passing to make this kind of withdrawal from the world, but it is one way in which a situation that seems to be beyond the control of anyone can be put back into the hands of the dying person themselves. It can become the responsibility of the terminally ill to ease their relatives' grief as well as to prepare themselves for progress in the afterlife.

It depends on the individuals involved, but I truly think that if the person who is ill can show that they are not afraid of the great event before them, they will significantly help those they leave behind. It's not healthy for either party to try and deny what is inevitable; if you accept the situation you can talk honestly about your lives together and settle issues which, if unresolved, might have complicated your grief with guilt or anger or confusion.

My Aunt Sylvia was a remarkable woman who'd lost a son to cancer and worked for years as a Macmillan nurse. She was so familiar with the stages of dying that when she was diagnosed with stomach cancer herself, she immediately set about dealing with her departure from this world, and easing the burden on her loved ones. She started to give away things that she wanted specific people to have and cleared up all sorts of emotional business. Privately, she also took a long hard look at her life and faced up to all her demons, all those times in her life when she hadn't been honest with herself or other people.

She was so good and thoughtful at doing this that when she

did eventually pass, everybody close to her took her death very calmly and hardly mourned at all. Anyone who'd visited her in the final days knew that she would be absolutely fine when she died. The only exception was my uncle Michael, her husband, who had never accepted that she would die. When she was lying in the hospice where she had herself worked, weighing barely four stone, he was still trying to assure her – or rather himself – that a cure was coming any day.

The dying are in a very sharp place mentally, and they take every word you say right into themselves. As they fade out of this world their minds become clearer in the next and they can see straight through you. Sylvia would have known that what Michael was telling her was nonsense but she could also see that he was nowhere near ready to let her go, and that was what made him come out with all this stuff.

This meant that she couldn't begin to talk to him about their lives together – he couldn't bear to listen as it would have meant that she was making her final goodbyes.

In the end she had to ask for my parents to take Uncle Michael gently out of the hospice before she could slip away. I'm sure one of the reasons he was so devastated by his bereavement was that his fear and denial meant that he wasn't ready to lose her, even when she was in great pain and in need of release.

CHAPTER FIVE

Why They Come Back

Why They Come Back

People often ask me why a lot of the messages the Spirits choose to pass on are so personal, and sometimes full of trivial bits of information, when they could be giving us next week's lottery numbers or the answer to that old chestnut about the meaning of life instead. The fact is that the chief purpose of those conversations with the other side is to reassure us about life after death. They have to convince us that they are still conscious and not only that they still have memories full of the tiny details and secrets of our lives on earth together but also that they are aware of what is happening to us now.

To this end they offer up scraps of information about illnesses they know we've endured since their passing, or even the fact that we've changed the wallpaper in the bathroom. They can give us precise dates or addresses, or describe a scene from the previous day. Usually messages this intricate come via mediums, but there are many ways that the Spirits use to communicate, and they certainly don't need a medium to do it.

I feel that everybody is clairvoyant and in theory open to

word from Spirit. We've all got a sixth sense and should use it, although it might take a bit of development. If you are aware of Spirit they will be able to reach you directly as you are, without the middleman. You may choose to see a medium at some point, but don't think that they are your only chance to hear from a loved one.

I have always tried to explain to people that when a Spirit person comes close to us we experience a sense of something strange, a feeling which tells us that something different is happening around us. The feeling of a Spirit being close to us is different from anything our mind can create and the feeling leaves us in no doubt that what we have received has touched our very soul.

Spirits can use the full range of human senses to reach us – sight, smell, touch, sound, even the sensation of taste. Spirits make themselves known to us in our dreams too, and when we're daydreaming – those times when we're a little spaced-out and out of focus.

In that state of mind we make room for our Spirit friends to get near to us as we open up and allow them in. The barriers created by 'being logical' and analysing our thoughts are down, and we're receptive to their messages. The trouble is when we snap to and try to write off the experience as wishful thinking. 'Of course I dreamt about him,' we think. 'I miss him; but that can't mean that he was actually *there*.' We'd rather think our subconscious was playing tricks on us or even that we were hallucinating than believe that our loved ones have been close to us.

For some, the creeping idea that maybe that was a communiqué from the other side provokes them to take steps to finding a medium. Others get signs that repeat themselves many times and become more and more persistent. When they are impossible to ignore, the recipient is often quick to find a good Spiritualist church in order to find out what on earth the other side has to say to them so urgently.

One of the best things that can happen in a sitting is that the message that I pass on to the living relative explains another experience that they've already had, and therefore confirms that their loved one has been in touch with them from the other side. For example, I once gave a reading to a girl whose brother had passed into Spirit following a car crash when he was travelling in Australia.

Partway through the sitting he suddenly said, 'Tell her it was me who gave her the coins' – which of course made no sense to me whatsoever. The expression on his sister's face told me that – if you'll forgive the pun – the penny had dropped. She grinned broadly and we went on with the session as her brother gave her more and more evidence and messages.

Afterwards we chatted and she told me all about the coins. It turned out that since her brother's death she had been finding stashes of Australian coins everywhere – in her car, her house, in different handbags and coats. They were real enough, and she couldn't work out where they were coming from, as her brother was the only person she knew who'd been to Australia.

Her brother was letting her know that he was still around and he only needed me as a medium to corroborate that for her, as of course I had no idea about what had been going on. That instant when she realized that her brother had been hiding the coins for her also reconnected the pair because now the sister knew that the bond between them had not been broken. Accepting that the link between them was still open meant that she had not lost her brother at all.

This kind of benevolent 'magician's trick' of making little objects appear in unlikely places is by no means common. Instead it seems that most often the departed use their family's and friends' dreams to communicate with them. Sadly those left behind usually have the vivid dreams in the immediate aftermath of the death, and because they are beside themselves with grief they dismiss them out of hand.

I knew a lady called Margaret Alexander who had been recently widowed and repeatedly dreamed of her husband. He'd be younger, and he always took her dancing, quite as they had in the early days of their marriage. She always woke up the next day feeling elated or even with laughter on her lips, only to be hit with the cold, dawning realisation that the man she had loved for so long was not with her any more. She was extremely rational about this and tried to put it out of her mind, only for the dream to recur, and the cycle of joy and disappointment made her sadder still.

Eventually she attended a Spiritualist church and a medium gave her a message from her husband, who protested that he didn't like the fact that she was doubting these experiences when he had put so much energy into creating them. For him it was a time when they could be together, and he could bring a smile back to her face. When Margaret understood this she was transformed, and the knowledge that the dance was real helped to lift her out of deep sorrow.

Sometimes the meaning of a dream can be less clear and takes a bit of figuring out. At a public demonstration I gave in America I gave a woman a message about a dream she had had. Her father came through to say that he had appeared to her as fit as a flea and skipping around like a mad thing, and that she found this more than a little nutty, as you would. After looking nonplussed for a second she confirmed that it was true, she *had* had that dream, and now that she thought about it she supposed he'd been trying to remind her of the way he'd been before his final, debilitating illness.

She'd been upset because she thought the way he was acting meant he'd somehow lost his marbles in the Spirit world, so she had ruled the dreams out as a mere quirk of her imagination. Hearing the message from her father at the demonstration changed her mind and she saw it all in another light. When she was a child her dad would mess around and act goofy to make her and her sister laugh – something she'd long since forgotten. Now she knew that her father had only been doing what he always did to cheer her up – clowning around.

Those in the Spirit world frequently communicate with their loved ones in ways which can seem awfully vague, yet when the Spirit has a chance to use a medium to reach their relatives they can confirm the message. Nine times out of ten they time these 'visits' to happen when the person left behind is at a particularly low point in life. They will make every effort to come through and if their relatives dismiss one attempt, they'll try again or look for another way in.

Creating a certain characteristic aroma is one of the most evidential ways a Spirit can use to identify themselves. It takes a great effort by the Spirit person to rearrange the very molecules of air around their loved one and those who've experienced the phenomenon have described it to me as a very intense experience that couldn't possibly have been imagined by them.

I once gave a private sitting to a mother and daughter who

had lost Joe, the father of the family. For months after his death they would both smell cigar smoke in their home, and sometimes the whiff of strong, fresh coffee. A coffee and a smoke had been Joe's favourite indulgences, and neither his widow nor his daughter had had them in the house since his passing.

I didn't know this or anything else about them when I began the session, and they cracked up when the first thing I said was that I was picking up the scent of cigars. Then the smell changed and I got coffee instead, and they laughed even harder. They knew for certain then that Joe was proving that he was still the man about the house, and it lifted their moods and reminded them of good times.

Naturally what people want most of all is to see an actual materialisation of the departed, or to hear their voice one more time. Both are high aims, and would cost a Spirit a great deal of effort to recreate. There have been cases of Spirits wholly or partially materialising, and they don't appear as shimmering visions or holograms but as fully three-dimensional beings. They're not lit up in some spooky kind of way but appear in the same light as their surroundings. The living person experiences them as being in the same physical room, not merely as mental images.

I'm not sure that this kind of miraculous occurrence is something to wish for, though. My friend the great medium Albert Best once saw a vision of his wife and children who had all been killed years before in the Second World War, and when acquaintances remarked that surely that had been a wonderful thing he could only shake his head. To him their apparition had been so vivid that when it faded it felt as though he had lost them all over again – a devastating experience.

You do need to be open-minded and receptive to let such messages come to you, but sometimes there is such a thing as trying too hard. When I was taking part in a development group at an early stage of my career there was a woman in the group who would see a small ball of light, just out of the corner of her eye every time she thought of her mother in the Spirit world. As soon as she turned her head to look at it head-on, it would vanish.

She complained to our mentor Mrs Primrose about how frustrating this was and Mrs P explained what was going on. She said that this was the mother's way of getting her daughter's attention and the chink of light would appear every time she queried whether her mum was still with her. When she strained round to see the manifestation it didn't disappear at all, but remained at the side of her vision, slightly out of focus.

There was no way of seeing it in full focus because it didn't exist there, so she would be no closer to sensing her mother's presence. Mrs Primrose advised her to relax and let the phenomenon be as it was – that was the only way she would learn to trust a message from the other world. If she constantly wanted it repeated and enlarged, she was only fuelling her own doubts and demanding more proof. This in turn closed down her awareness of her mother's presence and was making her gloomy as she thought she had lost her after all.

One of the hardest types of message to accept is what we call 'impressions' made by Spirit, which the receiver experiences as a strong urge to do something or an overwhelming sensation that the lost loved one is there with them – a sort of sudden emotional warmth and uplift. Because they are not visual or 'spelt out' by one of our senses but have to be felt instead, it can be hard to distinguish them.

As a medium I have had to learn to understand what are things impressed on my mind by a Spirit and what are merely my own thoughts and projections based on the desire to help people who are grieving. The best way to understand this is to guess what the purpose of the message was, as there is always a good reason that Spirits make the effort to cross the vale.

If it's something trivial like whether you should have a haircut or not, I doubt there's any Spirit involvement. The information you think you're being given by the departed should lie within the bounds of common sense and relate to truly important matters in your life. I'm not saying that Spirits don't impress thoughts on us just for the sake of it, but I'm dubious of a lot of the tales about a departed one hitching a lift on a loved one's life, as it were. It's more likely to be the overactive imagination of the living person.

It is true that our bond with departed loved ones is not broken, and that we can turn to them in times of trouble, but I get very uncomfortable when I hear about Spirits apparently dogging every step of their loved ones on earth. I get very sceptical. I once had a chat with an elderly gentleman who told me that although his wife had died over twenty years previously, she was with him constantly.

She told him what to wear and when to clean the house. She also gave him directions as he drove. I asked him if this Spirit satellite navigation always got him to his destination and he confided to me that actually, his dear departed wife had got it wrong recently, and sent him into a ditch on a dark night. He'd been pretty angry with her then, but had decided that she was teaching him a lesson because he hadn't listened earlier that day when she'd told him what to eat.

To me it was obvious 'she' wasn't a Spirit – Spirits seek to comfort and heal us, not boss us about and smack our wrists. This henpecking was self-inflicted as a way of papering over the great sadness he had felt, and still felt, at her death. There is a great difference between true Spirit intervention and the self-delusion that people create from loneliness or a severed emotional attachment, but it's rarely clear to the afflicted.

He was haunting himself, and I thought he could be happier if I brought a bit of common sense to the situation. This had to be delicately done, as clearly her 'voice' was a cornerstone of his life, though if 'she' kept giving duff directions like that he wasn't going to be around much longer!

I asked him to tell me when he first noticed the Spirit of his wife and he told me how at first he simply heard her voice talking to him just as she had done in life. Then she would come to him whenever he had to make the sort of decisions they had always discussed as a couple. He was still in the first few weeks of his grief and all he needed to do was talk to her and she'd respond in his head.

After this she began to take over his thinking and when he was alone she would sometimes even speak through him. I asked him if he had ever had an experience with his Spirit wife where he felt elated and lifted in a healing way and he told me he couldn't remember anything like that. Instead he said he had always felt exhausted after her visits. This told me the whole case was nothing to do with Spirit.

I also quickly worked out that he didn't want any explanation from me about the real situation and that whatever I suggested, his mind was made up. It was his darling wife who would not let *him* go and not the other way round. He had spent twenty years elaborately creating this scenario and there was nothing I could do to unravel it in the short space of time I had without sending him into shock at losing 'her' all over again. He needed counselling, but I doubted he'd ever seek it. He was certainly in his own realm of reality now.

Often people who get caught up in this kind of fantasy are merely afraid to let go in case they lose contact altogether, but that's not possible. Frequently they think that by clinging to their lost one they are preventing their progression in the Spirit world, but that's also impossible as I've made clear. Ironically, they are holding themselves back because their grief does not evolve and become easier to cope with, but has been swept under the carpet and denied instead.

Those in the Spirit world would never set out to cause such an imbalance in our minds, and would probably not manifest themselves if they believed doing so could lead their loved one into delusion. If a mind does not know itself, the Spirit cannot begin to get through to the person and transmit their true message of compassion or healing.

They are very sensitive to what we need and know when the time is right for their grieving relatives to feel their presence around them, and when it will only cause them more sorrow. There is a natural law in the Spirit world which often prevents them from coming back to us because it is understood on the other side that their doing so might hold us back instead of assisting us. It was unlikely that the wife of the gentleman with the 'Spirit' satellite navigation would actually visit him, as in his confusion he might have taken her arrival as confirmation that he'd been right to listen to the false voice for so long.

Word from Spirit should not become a crutch for those living in the world nor an oracle to be consulted every time we have difficulty making up our minds. That kind of notion would take away the true purpose of Spirit communication and devalue it for those who have already been given help.

It's common for Spirits to combine mental impressions with what I'd call 'synchronicity'. This is essentially a pattern of coincidences that seems too significant to be random and can take all manner of forms. Perhaps when you're having one of those sudden lows that seem to come out of nowhere and start missing your loved one intensely, you are aware that 'your' song will start playing on the radio, or a snatch of it will blast out of the window of a passing car.

A friend of mine who lost her mother missed her desperately and one day shortly after her death she was sitting alone in her living room weeping as she'd done many times in the last few weeks. Inwardly she was desperately begging her mum for a sign, when the phone rang and made her start. She picked it up but after a short chat the woman at the other end realized she'd got the wrong number and rang off. For no particular reason Jackie dialled 1471 to see who had called and realized with a shock that the woman had phoned her from her mother's old number.

It could be a freak coincidence or it could be synchronicity – just Jackie's ma's way of getting in touch. Jackie chose not to be hard on herself and pass it off as chance, but understood that her mum had been somehow tinkering with the switchboard from the other side. I think most of the letters I receive from readers are looking for confirmation that this type of phenomenon really is word from their loved ones – and I expect that there are as many ways of getting that hint across as there are Spirits.

Those who claim to have experienced such a happening want it to be their Spirit person more than anything and very often I would have to conclude that it could well be them. It is, however, a little unhealthy to believe that radio DJs pick out their play lists solely because they're influenced by Spirits on the other side or that every twinge in your ankle means that Aunt Doris is trying to tell you you'll fall over next week. It's more likely that you're wearing the wrong shoes, and then you probably *will* take a tumble.

There's another dimension to synchronicity, and that's that in my experience it is always exactly the right time for the best messages to come through to a loved one. By this I mean that the sitter must be in the right mental state to hear the message, and not too distraught to accept it straightforwardly. If we leave it to the Spirit to judge that the time is right for those words of comfort to come through, they tend to be more accurate and more healing. Getting the moment right involves a synchronisation of a whole chain of events that plays out either for the sitter or myself, or sometimes even for both of us and a bunch of other people too!

I always remember a lady called Jenny who had asked me if she could have a private sitting a few days after her father had passed over. I immediately felt that I had to say no – it wasn't that I was too busy or didn't want to help, but more as though I was getting a strong signal from Spirit that I shouldn't. A short time later Jenny appeared in my salon and asked me again. Once more I said no, as I didn't think the time was right. Nothing from Spirit was coming through, but I experienced instead the sensation that my mind was emptying, as though I couldn't think of anything at all just after she'd asked. I felt awful, but had to be honest as the sitting would have been a mere charade if nobody on the other side had anything to say.

About six months later I went on a cruise on the Mediterranean with my friend for a nice relaxing holiday. It was only our second night on board when I did a double take and all but rubbed my eyes – Jenny was standing next to me in her uniform. She was a stewardess on the boat. It was a new posting and she'd joined the ship only the previous day. We greeted each other and laughed about the coincidence, and went our separate ways.

The next day, however, I caught up with her on one of the decks and arranged for her to have a sitting when she was next off duty and I'd finished sunning myself. I no longer had that mental blank, and knew that her father wanted to come through, which he did almost as soon as we sat down for the session. He described lots of important things that had happened to his family since his death, which he could never have given as proof if we'd talked the first time Jenny came to see me.

He said that his wife had just come through an operation to remove her breast and the cancer that lay within. He told Jenny that he was standing beside his wife all through her operation and even gave her the exact name of the surgeon who had performed the procedure. The most important thing to my mind was that he said he would not have come through earlier as he could not tell Jenny anything positive and hopeful as he knew that his wife would have this diagnosis.

Now that she was recovering and Jenny was back at work he could comfort them and share with them the joy he wanted them to understand he was experiencing in Spirit now that he was free from all the physical pain he had endured when he was in his body. He ended by passing news to his daughter about her mother and a private little message that he said would give her hope for the rest of her life.

That was enough for Jenny and she didn't ask me for any more readings. When we bumped into each other on the ship we chatted and she told me she was completely convinced that her father had staged everything and when she'd called her mother she'd agreed that he was somehow behind everything. I told her that she was just one of many whose loved ones on the other side knew best when to deliver a message and that I couldn't force them to do it if they had other plans.

Only Spirits really know when the time is right and, indeed, if it will serve any purpose. By allowing myself to trust the Spirit I've been shown more times than not that when there *is* a message for someone, that message will reach them by hook or by crook. Sometimes the timing is dramatic in the extreme, and it can be life- saving. Albert Best had an astonishing story about this.

He'd been on a long trip to India and returned to his little flat in Glasgow two days later than expected – something had muddled up his travel arrangements. He'd only been home for a few minutes and hadn't even started to unpack when there was a knock on the door. He opened it to find a stranger standing outside. When Albert told me the story he said that one look in this man's eyes told him he desperately needed help, and so he didn't hesitate to invite him in and sit him down in the living room.

He sat down opposite him and tuned straightaway into the Spirit world, following a gut feeling that someone needed to reach him as soon as possible.

A woman came through and told Albert that she was the stranger's wife, gave him her name and the fact that she had recently gone over after a long battle with breast cancer. The stranger accepted this information and was eager to know what else Albert could relay. His wife, it seemed, was mainly concerned with his dire emotional state and she said that he was not coping with her death and their son was also in a bad way. After almost an hour of messages she asked Albert to tell the man that he must not take the tablets he had left on the bathroom shelf at home, at which the husband collapsed in tears, saying, 'It was her I heard! She knows! She really knows!'

When she had finished all she needed to say, Albert sat alone with the man for a long time and he told the medium how sick he had been with grief after his wife passed. He'd felt hollow, and not even the thought of his beloved son still living could haul him out of that misery. His doctor had sent him on a course of counselling, but that had had no effect. As a last resort he'd been to a Spiritualist church, hoping against hope that his wife would come through but nothing came of it.

He thought long and hard about his life and earlier on the day he went to see Albert he had sat in the bathroom counting out pills and resolving to take his own life. Out of the blue he heard his wife calling out 'No!' to him as loudly as though she was in the room with him. He was still reeling from the shock when the phone rang and he picked it up to hear a woman he'd met at the Spiritualist church informing him that the highly respected medium Albert Best had returned from a trip to India and that he should try to see him for a private sitting. I don't think she meant he should see him then and there, but the man was so distressed that that was exactly what he did – unknowingly timing his arrival perfectly.

He apologized to Albert for the intrusion but explained that he had made a pact with himself that if it really had been his wife calling out to him then she would be able to talk to him through the medium and prove that she was still alive in Spirit. If nothing came of his attempt to see Albert, then he would go straight home and take those piles of pills to end his suffering. Her voice had been so real to him that he was ready to bet his life on the message.

Albert wouldn't even have been in Glasgow had his return not been delayed – he was supposed to be visiting London but that trip was cancelled when he got back from India late. When Albert first told me the tale I only looked at how consummate his mediumship had been for the names and accurate details he had been able to obtain. Now I look at the work of Spirit in bringing it all about and how events were synchronized to bring this poor man a much-needed healing.

Albert and he became good friends and I later met the man, who has confirmed the story to me. His son also had sittings with Albert and was able to communicate with his mother from time to time. He and his father came to terms with the physical loss of a lady who loved them both so much, but spiritually they now knew in their hearts that she was always with them.

Sometimes the person on the receiving end of a synchronistic experience isn't even looking for a communication in the first place, which doesn't bother the Spirits a bit. In the time that I've been a medium I've always been aware that there are many people out there who, for whatever reason, do not wish to investigate the idea of life after death.

This is entirely their prerogative and I would never foist a reading on someone who really didn't want to hear it. There have only been a few occasions when an unsought message has come through for someone who happened to be in proximity to me at the time, but I always gave them the option of hearing the details or not. As it happens, on each of these occasions the recipient ended up being convinced of the continued existence of their loved one, and was grateful to have heard from them.

Once I took part in a radio interview in London, and when we were done one of the production team was given the task of walking me from the studio to my car. We'd just got into the lift when I heard the voice of a woman in the Spirit world telling me that she was happy. I looked at the young producer standing opposite me and wondered if I should say anything to her. The idea of dishing out this news made me very uncomfortable as I'd rather someone comes to me looking for help. She might be a bit freaked-out to be trapped in a lift with a weird medium telling her the dead wanted a word, too.

Looking for reassurance I sent out a thought to the Spirit person asking who she was and she swiftly replied that she was the woman's mother and her energy was so strong that I blurted out loud, 'Your mother is here and wants you to know she is happy.' The producer looked shocked, but couldn't fight her curiosity. She asked softly if there was anyone with her mother, and I heard a man's voice cut in and say he was her father. When I told the producer her hand shot to her mouth.

She asked only one more question – 'Do they know they have a grandson?' I never even had to relay that to the Spirits – it came right out of my mouth as though her father had spoken through me. 'Yes, we know you have a little boy.' With this the young woman shed a tear and her expression became ecstatic. As the lift door opened she hugged me and said she would never have believed such a thing was possible and that she hadn't thought of going to a medium.

I told her I wasn't in the habit of giving messages to people who don't ask for them but her parents had taken the chance and I followed the impression I got from them. I had to trust the Spirit world and they were, as always, right. She told me that when her son was born a few weeks after her father's death she had experienced a deep sadness that neither of her parents would ever know they had a grandson. The communication was brief, but it told her all she needed to know.

Sometimes synchronicity can be so fluky that it's almost comical and when you factor in more than one 'sensitive', the Spirit-driven plot can lead you on what feels like a wild goose chase, when you're least expecting it. I've written in my previous books about my friend Dronma who is a Tibetan Buddhist and a psychic artist. Synchronicity loves Dronma, and if she phones you up and asks you to follow her on some whim or another, you know something interesting is going to happen.

Recently I had a friend staying with me at my house near Loch Lomond. The scenery is stunning and the weather was holding up well for Scotland, so we thought we'd have a day out in the Trossachs, a national park full of beautiful lochs and glens. I still laugh about this, because I can't believe how hard the Spirits must have been working to bring everything about and get the timing spot-on.

So Dronma phoned from Stirling and said we should meet up and drive in convoy to a special place she felt the need to visit. Now Dronma might be a Buddhist, but she's not some demure, mousey person – she's very intuitive and active in her compassion. Everything gets done on the spur of the moment and I've learned to follow that. When we met up with her that day she announced, 'I'm going to take you to the Wish Tree.' I said, 'Oh, right. *Where* exactly are we going now?' and she told me to stop asking questions and just follow. So we set off behind her.

Nothing was straightforward about the drive, as it rarely is with Dronma. She had her two huge dogs hopping around in the back of the car making chaos, and she also smokes as she drives – it's the one thing she hasn't been able to renounce for her faith. Food, booze, material goods, yes; but fags, no. We'd gone a few miles when she suddenly stopped and hopped out of the car to rummage in the back. When I asked what was going on she said she thought the cigarette she'd chucked out the window had blown back into the car and might set the dogs on fire. It took a while to check that her fears were ungrounded and they weren't all going to go up in a puff of petrol and dog hair.

Then our little caravan started up again and on we went until we passed a garden centre, and Dronma took a swift right into the car park. 'I saw a dragon,' she said. 'Let's go in and have a look.' Right, I thought, we'll never get to the Wish Tree at this rate. After an hour or so of pottering around the garden statuary section we all piled back into the cars and carried on.

Eventually we arrived at a wood in Aberfoyle, parked the cars and climbed up a hill to a big gnarled oak tree covered in ribbons. People write their wishes on scraps of ribbon and tie them onto the tree, and apparently the fairies will then come and take them away and try to help. It's a very still, calm place with a lovely quiet energy.

We were taking in the atmosphere and admiring the tree when we heard someone approaching. It sounded like a family with children, and this is how spiritual we were feeling that day – we all groaned at the thought that the peace would be shattered! I suppose we still hadn't learned that 'spiritual' isn't necessarily about being terribly reverent and lighting candles and all that.

The family hoved into view, and turned out to be a grandmother and her two grandchildren. She came up to chat and said that she had brought the children to make a wish at the tree because their father had died. She'd told them that the tree was magical and their wishes might well come true.

When the kids had made their wishes they wandered over to where we stood chatting and the grandmother winked at me and said, 'You're magic, aren't you?' and I played along and said,

'Yes, I'm magic.' Then she asked Dronma in turn and Dronma assured the little boy and girl that she was magic too. The girl looked at me very spryly and said, 'Nanna, that's Gordon Smith, that man whose book you're reading.' And her nanna blinked at me and said, 'Oh, my God!'

The girl then asked me about her father and where he was, and I took off the little Mayan calendar I was wearing as a pendant and gave it to her. I told her, 'Whenever you want your daddy and don't feel close to him you should hold this, and then you'll feel him. You may not see or hear him but you'll know he's there.' Her grandmother thanked us and we carried on chatting. She then mentioned that after their father's death she had found some relief from her pain by going on a retreat to a Buddhist temple in the Scottish countryside. She raved about the amazing images painted in the temple and said she really wanted to meet the person who had created them because they had helped her so much, and I grinned and said, 'Well, here she is', as I knew the temple and that its wonderful paintings were the work of Dronma.

By now the synchronicities were piling up so fast there was nothing to do but laugh in astonishment, and we weren't a bit surprised by the time it turned out that the lady had been trying to get tickets to a book reading I was doing and hadn't been able to lay hands on them. We weren't surprised, because of course my visiting friend was my publisher, and she was able to arrange a place for the lady at the reading.

We finally parted ways, and as my party walked off down the hill there was a moment of perfect stillness when we heard the lady say to her grandchildren, 'I told you we'd find magic, and isn't that real magic?' and for a moment that was absolutely what it felt like. I thought, 'Yes, there really is magic, and you don't need to have an apparition or some sort of firework for it to happen.' I hope those kids do believe in magic now, and keep that part of their minds open as they grow. I can't imagine anything more healing for such young people who had suffered such losses so early.

CHAPTER SIX

Messages of Hope

Messages of Hope

Another art that Spirits have that can seem to us like magic is their ability to look into our futures. There is no time in Spirit, so it might be better to say that they are simply aware of a broader field of events than we are. In folk stories and dramas Spirits are forever pitching up to make dire warnings to the living so that they can cheat destiny and save themselves from an awful fate. I know of several examples of people who were warned about something by Spirits of their departed relatives, but not in the way you might think.

I was once approached at a residential course by a woman whose long-dead husband had appeared to her in a dream and held her close to him. She said the feeling had been 'Out of this world; I can't really describe how intense and wonderful it was.' In the dream her husband had told her not to worry about their son Mark. She thought this was because Mark worked abroad and she often worried about him, as mums do. The dream left her feeling relaxed and soothed.

Two days later she was telephoned by her son to say that he

had had an accident at work and been taken to hospital, but he was fine now. No-one had told her earlier because he had wanted to be the one to reassure her in person. Her heart leapt into her mouth but then she remembered her husband's message and calmed down once more. Everything would be ok, and he was looking out for their son even when it was impossible for her to do so.

You see, the point of the communication was not to intervene with the course of events and save her son from injury, but to make sure that she wouldn't be sent into a spiralling panic at the news and imagine all sorts of nasty outcomes. I would say that this is generally how Spirits intervene – it is our emotional wellbeing that they have the power to alter.

If our Spirit friends could change fate, I suppose we'd heed their warnings and never have any life experiences that weren't good or fortunate. That's just not how the human existence works – it is in Spirit that we are finally freed from physical and emotional restraints that cause us such pain. I wish I could prevent suffering by giving messages, but when the Spirits use me to console their loved ones it is just that – a way of easing their distress and not preventing it in the first place.

I was doing a demonstration at a Spiritualist church and among the communications and pieces of evidence that came through were some from a husband to his wife in the audience.

Six months later I was at another such meeting when the same woman approached me, this time highly distressed. She said she had to know, 'Why didn't my husband tell me he was coming to take our granddaughter? He said nothing about that. Why didn't he tell me she would die weeks later?'

Her little granddaughter had become very sick and died within a short time and the family were devastated. It was natural that she wanted to know that her husband had been there to welcome the child, but though I knew she must be frantic with sadness, there was only one answer I could give her. 'Would you have wanted to hear that she would die? Do you think your husband would have wanted you to have that horrendous knowledge, even if he could pass it on?' What sort of torture would her family have gone through, living two dread months in the knowledge that the girl would be taken from them?

She insisted that her husband had mentioned a date and that it had been the day before the little girl's suffering ended, but again I had to quash that thought. If it had been the exact date then it would have been some kind of reassurance related to the girl's passing, but as it was not, it must be connected to something else. Sometimes it can take years to solve the mystery of a date given to us by the Spirits.

This was not what the lady wanted to hear, and I knew she must have had a harrowing time since the child took ill, turning the thought over and over in her mind and wondering why her husband hadn't warned her. All I could do was to try and comfort her and reiterate what I am trying to say in this book – that the bond of love that exists between us on this earth is not broken by the move to Spirit, and that our loved ones are only trying to spare us as much sorrow as they can.

It was not the case that I had somehow received more information from his Spirit and decided to censor the details myself – a medium shouldn't and indeed probably couldn't do that. Occasionally we are aware of more information, but this is hedged by a strong sense from the Spirit not to convey it to their loved one – those on the other side make the choice of what is to be known on earth, not us mediums. We're not seers, but more like instruments for Spirit use when we open our minds for them to express their concern or affection for their families and friends.

I was sure her husband was there when her granddaughter passed, and I was sure he was with her now as she grieved. Sometimes they judge that it is better to protect us from information about the future than plunge us into the knowledge that something inescapable but gruelling is looming on the horizon.

It's not rare for a message to arrive sideways, as it were. If the Spirit's relative doesn't see a medium themselves, it may be that a medium finds him- or herself delivering a message to a friend of theirs, with the instruction to pass it on. This happened to me when I was just beginning to explore the Spiritualist tradition, some twenty years ago. It was the first time I ever saw Albert Best in action, and got a first-hand experience of his matter-of-fact way of delivering messages.

About halfway through the demonstration Albert said, 'There's someone who's sitting at the back of this church who knows someone who is dying of Aids.' Now this was 1985, and there was a colossal prejudice against the disease. I felt uncomfortable because I knew he meant me – I knew Stuart, who was in hospital in the final stages of the illness. He was a friend of my colleague Christine, and of her brother whose death in a fire resulted in one of my first mediumistic experiences as an adult. That week Christine had asked me if I would go and see Stuart in order to give him a shave, and I'd put off the favour for a few days, having too much else on my plate.

The whole congregation was busy looking round to see who'd admit to knowing this man – people were still very ignorant then – and eventually I put my hand up. 'Yes, you,' said Albert, unfazed, as everyone twisted round to stare at me. 'You've got to go and shave him because you're a barber.' 'Yes,' he carried on, 'but you won't have to because he'll be dead in four days. Incidentally, there's a man called Brian here who died in a fire and it's his sister who asked you to do this. Could you pass a message to his sister?' 'Yes. I know her.' 'Yes, you do. He was an electrician. He's telling you he's sorry he couldn't get through to her but he's so glad she's going to have a baby.' This was news to me! Albert continued, 'He's here for Stuart too, when he passes. Oh, and you? Have a good time in Florida.'

I did pass on the news to Christine, who was amazed because she was in the very early stages of her pregnancy and hadn't told anyone. She later had a private reading with Albert where Brian came through to give her more messages. He was right about Stuart too, sadly, as he passed over before I could keep my appointment with him, just four days later.

I've heard many tales from people I've met over the years about all kinds of wonderful phenomena, but I think one of the most beautiful and strange stories concerning Spirit communication is this one, which came to light when I gave a private sitting to a lady called Anne a few years ago. It began before she'd even sat down to begin the session; as she crossed the room to shake my hand in greeting, I was suddenly aware of a large white feather floating down from the ceiling. I hadn't even composed myself and tuned into Spirit when I said out loud, 'This is a gift from your son. He sends you them all the time.' Now I felt really stupid saying that, because we hadn't even introduced ourselves to each other and here I was gabbing away very unprofessionally without even going via my own Spirit guides.

Her son wasn't bothered about the proper channels, though; he just went on to tell her that he wanted her to keep all the feathers and that he would keep sending them. 'What?' I thought. 'How many of these feathers has she got?' But I kept shtoom and left my mind open for Todd to come through. As Anne and I sat together for an hour or so he passed on more pieces of evidence and words of comfort for his mother, who received them calmly, with a quiet smile on her face.

When the time had come for us to finish, I had a few questions of my own, and soon Anne had told me the whole story. Todd had taken his own life at the young age of eighteen, and none of his family had been able to fathom why he had felt so desperate and alone. In the course of the sitting he was able to explain why, and it was the most heart-wrenching reason. He had realized he was gay and thought, mistakenly, that he couldn't cope with this knowledge. He had taken himself off away from his family and killed himself, and the first they knew of his despair was when the police arrived to break the news.

When his poor, baffled mother was given a plastic bag full of Todd's things by the police she was mystified to see a large white feather in with his wallet and watch. The policewoman who handed them over couldn't explain where it had come from. Since then, there had been a flurry of feathers. If Anne took her car to be cleaned, when she collected it she would find a feather in the glove compartment.

They tumbled out of thin air to land on her shoulder when she was sitting by herself in her bedroom. She'd be unpacking the shopping and find one in a kitchen cupboard. Hardly knowing why she did it, she kept them all, first in an envelope and then, when that overflowed, in a box. She realized gradually that there was a pattern to the materialisations – the feathers always appeared when she was deep in thought about her son and wondering what awful emotions he must have been going through at the time of his suicide.

By the time she came to see me she said she had enough feathers to stuff a duvet, or, she joked, make wings and fly away. She knew in her heart that these were from Todd, and it was my mention of the feathers that let her believe in the rest of the messages that he conveyed via me. She was instinctively sceptical about the notion of life after death, but what she had seen with her own eyes gave her faith.

It was Todd's way of letting her know that whatever agonies he had undergone when he decided to end his life he was not suffering now and that she must think of him as happy, not tortured. I see Anne occasionally and she tells me she keeps getting white feathers from Todd, a gentle reminder that he's still around and a symbol of hope.

CHAPTER SEVEN

How We Die

How We Die

Sceptics accuse mediums of using a technique called 'cold reading', which involves watching a person's body language for clues and surreptitiously asking them questions which will give the fake medium more ammunition. Just how the way someone blinks is supposed to tell me their exact address, I don't know, but the kind of evidence I am able to offer the bereaved is far too precise for me to be making lucky guesses. I don't sit around going, 'You live at number one, Acacia Avenue. No? Number two? No? Number three?' and so on.

I've taken part in experiments by scientists to test what I'm doing, and even when I had anonymous sitters who were in a different room I was able to convey names and dates and other descriptions to them, despite having no physical contact with them whatsoever. I don't think I need to prove any more that it is the Spirit world who are using me to contact their loved ones at that time.

Usually, though, I meet people face-to-face in more normal surroundings, and you don't need psychic awareness to be able to guess what sort of loss they have suffered. I've met so many people at various stages of grief that I can recognize their symptoms now. You can call it cold reading if you like, but I don't let my intuition overrule the communications I get from the Spirit world. It's just that you can tell from someone's posture, even, what they have endured.

Being able to sense myself the very deep need and feelings of helplessness which these people often give off is a spur to try to do my best to change things for them. If nobody comes through or they seem to have difficulty accepting a message, I feel very bad myself.

A medium can't help but notice these different signs as it's part of the building of empathy which is required between them and the sitter if the sitting is to be successful. For years I didn't realize that I was picking up these sorts of signals from the people who came to see me and thought that everything I was thinking was coming from the Spirit world. If I'd realized this I would have felt like a fraud at the time, but now I realize that there are many factors all working at the same time when I use my gift, and every aspect of it – psychic or otherwise – is important to what I do.

It's difficult to generalize about these signs of grief, as obviously all deaths are different and all individuals experience their loss in different ways and at different times in their own life, when they might be more or less able to cope. However, there are some things that recur again and again, because more often than not the manner in which a person died dictates how their loved ones will handle mourning.

People who have lost someone after a long illness display a mixture of emotions. On the one hand, the experience of watching their loved one be slowly sapped of health has left them with a certain resignation and pessimism. On the other hand, they tend to be more mentally alert than others as they already began grieving as their loved one faded. They've had time to prepare for their loss and to set things straight, and I think that if the deceased was very sick indeed, there is a sense of relief too, as the mourners knew that they had to let go of their loved one so that they could be out of pain.

Similarly, people who have lost someone of old age generally cope well – probably best of all. It is seen as a 'natural death' and if they pass in their sleep, those left behind can take comfort from the fact that they didn't suffer at the end of a long physical life. The process of mourning seems to move smoothly, and those on earth don't need word from the other side so desperately.

Once when I was working at the SAGB an old boy in his eighties came in. He looked very frail, but I could tell he was not a man who was weighed down by grief. When we got a communication from his wife, the whole story of her death emerged, and it was very moving. She had been ill for some time and on a life-support machine, and the doctors had said someone must take the decision to switch it off and let her pass over.

The old man, Ted, had insisted that he must be the only person to do that, and that was why he came to see a medium. He just needed to know that what he had done was right by his wife at the end of her life. She came through to say, 'I knew you could do it, darling,' and his eyes lit up. He told her, 'I was never afraid for you,' and she just responded, 'I knew you would do it.'

As she lay between life and death she had been impressing on his mind that he must release her, and he had only worried that she might have wanted their children to make the choice and not him. As he'd done it, he'd tried to send out a thought to her of 'I'm doing this for you, darling,' and it had obviously reached her. When the session was over he told me that he was happy she had gone, as, 'We'd done all our loving in this world. I couldn't ask for any more love in my life than I had with this woman.'

This was typical of the sort of reaction most people have to losing someone of old age, as was the rest of the message that she sent to him. She let him know that she had been reunited with other family members and she signed off, as it were, a rich life. You shouldn't assume, though, that just because someone reaches a ripe old age, their relatives can come to terms with the loss.

There may be other levels of emotion which underlie the grief and cause genuine depression to form and prolong the mourning.

To understand grief we need to understand the person who is bereaved, though getting to the bottom of some people's personalities and lives would take longer than a half-hour sitting. Some people remain a mystery, despite their emotional outpourings at the time.

A face sticks in my mind, a man who told me he was seventy-eight years old and came to me in a very bad way indeed because he said he had to have a message from his mother in the Spirit world. She had died peacefully several weeks before I met him, only a few months short of her hundredth birthday. A good innings!

Her son was inconsolable, though, and teary throughout the sitting. He protested that she'd left him all alone when she'd said that she'd always be there for him. It was one of those times when nothing much comes through from the Spirit world, so I tried to console him. He clung to my hands and demanded that I get his mother for him; I wanted to help, but the Spirit world had its own reasons for keeping quiet.

He came looking for me a few more times at Spiritualist talks, insisting that we fix an appointment for another private reading. He said he'd kill himself if he couldn't get a connection to his mother, but his threats had no effect. There was nothing coming through from her. The last time I saw him he had been referred to a counsellor but was still very depressed.

It must have been a year or so later when I was at the Spiritualist church where I first met the man that I was told by the church secretary that he had indeed taken his life, as he'd thought no-one could help him. I still think about him, years later, as I can never fathom the nature of his attachment to his mother and how he'd felt he couldn't live without her.

Self-pity had made him look on death as a personal attack on him, rather than the release of a very tired, very old lady from this life into the Spirit world. I think he can never have considered the fact that she would, in all likelihood, die before him, but just put those thoughts as far out of mind as he could. To him it had been a sudden, unexpected death.

I can always tell people who have lost a loved one suddenly, whether from a heart attack, accident or a violent means. They are physically on edge and jumpy, as though they're waiting for the next blow to strike. They show a mixture of disbelief at the death and an urgent need to have the afterlife existence of their loved one confirmed.

At the SAGB I once gave a sitting to a woman who was somewhere in her thirties and as soon as she sat down it was as though she had to hold herself to the seat to keep herself from pacing round the room. Nothing about her was relaxed, despite my best efforts to put her at her ease. Her knuckles were white as she gripped the arms of the chair.

I gave her the first piece of evidence from her brother who told me that he had died suddenly. Nobody had known he had any health problems, so his death at a young age had been completely out of the blue. When his sister heard that first confirmation she loosened her grip a little, but then tensed to wait for the next thing. I felt as though she was willing me to bring her more, and every time I paused she was back at the edge of her seat.

Things came through for their mother too, who had been devastated, and an absolutely accurate time for the man's death. This accuracy is needed all the more for those who are in this kind of shock as they need the evidence both to bring home to them what has happened and that their loved one is still with them. When the brother offered more trivial things I could see her look disappointed, only to edge her chair closer when the more crucial things came through. I don't think she realized what she was doing, but she was practically in my lap by the time she'd had enough evidence to be satisfied.

People in the same situation as this lady all have this outward fidgety behaviour, but what is most striking is that inside them there's a quietness that's unnatural. For a sensitive the silence is almost deafening, and it pulls you in. You can talk to them and it's almost as though your words fall headlong into that silence like it's a pit. Then the words strike something deep in them, and suddenly you have their full attention.

With people who haven't lost someone suddenly, it's possible to talk on an ordinary level. You don't get the sensation that they haven't taken in half of what you are trying to tell them. The hardest people to try to reach are those whose loved one took their own life. They have an air of total defeat.

They also have more questions left unanswered which weigh heavily on them. Unlike people whose loved ones were killed in an accident, they don't necessarily feel absolved from blame even when their child or partner tells them the suicide was not their fault. When they get the explanation for that person's despair, you can see them almost crumble as they try to see how they could have known it, and said the right things at the right time.

I often try to do some healing above and beyond the mediumship for these people and to persuade them that they could not have done anything differently. People die when they are meant to die, and not for all the 'I-should-have-knowns' or missed opportunities would they be saved. In this life we have a start point and an end point, and what we do between those two markers is up to us – I suppose you could say that some people take the scenic route. If you have prevented someone from killing themselves once, only for them to take their own life eventually, all that means is that both those things were meant to happen.

It's your human mind that wonders endlessly about the way their future life might have been, if they'd married or had children or you'd said that thing you meant to say to them. If you accept that their time here just reached its natural end, you can see them in a better light. The best thing to do is to deal with your guilt and try to move on, the better to send positive thoughts to the suicide, who will need them in order to progress.

As you might expect, people whose relatives or friends have been torn from them by someone else's violence have a whole other side to their grief. They also have that defeated air, but it's backed by an anger that's like a third presence in the room. They try to bite it back, though, and conceal it with a simple need to know more about their loved one and how they died.

I was working in the USA when I met a couple who had come to see a medium together. They were both smartly dressed, but had the air of not being comfortable in their best clothes, which seemed strange. It was as though they were dressing up their own suppressed fury as the simple desire to hear from their lost relative. The man was rigid with anger throughout our half hour together, in contrast to the woman, who was limp with defeat.

When I tuned in and was immediately able to tell them,

'Your son was murdered,' the mother began to cry and the father started wiping his eyes. He swore under his breath and the woman took his arm, trying to hold him back so that she could get the message she desperately needed. I tried to be as gentle as possible as I passed on the information their son showed me.

He had been stabbed and thrown into a river in a dodgy part of the city and the newspapers had speculated on his death in a particular way that the son said was not true. He offered words of comfort that his mother received gratefully, and I could see her finding strength in the fact that her son was still with her and happy. The father barely took this on board, and wanted to quiz the son about his killers: 'Did you see them? What did they look like?' Every fibre of his body was intent on having the answers.

This the young man couldn't convey, and I had to try to break it to the father that I could give him evidence that his son wasn't suffering, but I could not give him justice, and neither could the son in the afterlife, it seemed. At the end the father told me, 'What you've done for my wife is good.' I said that he too must have had something worthwhile from it and he paused, as though he were reining in that same rage and reminding himself to be polite. His wife touched his arm again, anxiously. Then he said, 'Yes, thank you. You have helped me, but I still want to kill those people.'

When a murder is unresolved in this way it's understandable

that the bereaved turn to the Spirit world for answers. After all, they have a far greater knowledge of these things than us on earth, but there can be no guarantee of it. What a medium tries to offer is a healing for the loved ones of the victim, as the victim himself is beyond harm now. It's their family and friends who are grievously injured.

Often they don't want the world to see how deeply they have been stung by the loss, nor that they've been turned bitter by it, but it's as good as written on their faces. Hatred becomes a mental trap, even when it seems justified. If everything you do is consumed by that negative drive, it cannot be good for you or those around you. I have known people to overcome the murder of a loved one and turn their suffering into something positive, but this takes an extraordinary spiritual effort. Here, perhaps, more than ever, if you can come to understand the Spirit world you will find it easier to come to terms with the heart-wrenching bereavement.

A violent death or suicide leaves such a stain on the mind of those left to mourn because of its very nature. It's impossible for them not to torture themselves with trying to imagine what it was like for the victim to be so afraid and to suffer unthinkable physical injuries. They want to know and share their pain, and the knowledge that they didn't prevent it happening makes them feel inadequate.

I think this same inadequacy is intensified in the case of parents who have lost young children. Any parent is duty-bound to look after their child and protect them from the worst the world can throw at them, so when a turn of events snatches that from their hands, the feeling of helplessness is overwhelming. Yet more than any other type of communication I have given, it's almost always those that involve children that seem to be more successful and beneficial to the recipients than any other.

I believe that the connection between young children and their parents is very spiritual and instinctive; in particular there's a true telepathy between mothers and their kids and that makes the link strong when they have passed over to the other side. I believe that the vitality and innocence of children help the communication too, because their young minds are uncomplicated and the messages which they pass are much more animated and full of life.

I travelled to northern Italy to give a series of private readings a few years ago and saw a couple who were barely in their thirties. I supposed because of this that they had lost a child. When a couple suffer such a loss it seems that they are either bonded closer together because no-one else can understand what they have gone through, or the relationship is blown apart because they grieve differently, and cannot understand each other's different reactions.

This couple were obviously united in grief, but the man was putting a braver face on things in order to protect his wife. His whole body language was directed toward his wife, who was openly distraught. He watched her constantly, sitting with his arm protectively round her shoulders, and every time I gave them some new piece of information via the translator he would give her a squeeze to make sure that she knew he was there for her.

They had indeed lost a child, a little boy of ten. I gave them his name and the wife gulped, but the husband still remained focused on her. The boy and his entire class had been killed when they were out skiing, when an avalanche had swept down the mountain and buried them all. The next proof the boy gave was to name every one of his friends who had passed with him, and at each mention the woman brightened, knowing that it was her son who was coming through.

The pivotal moment came when the little boy gave me a message just for his father. He thanked him for playing a particular Italian pop song at his funeral – I gave the translator some of the lyrics and she sang a few lines to the couple, and at this the father's whole demeanour changed. He gave way totally – you could feel the emotion swelling his chest – and it was his wife's turn to support him instead.

I can't speak Italian, but it was obvious they were ecstatic.

The translator told me later that they were repeating over and over to each other how glad they were that the child was not alone, but with his friends. I think this was the best news that I could give them, but it was also significant that the boy acknowledged what they had done at his funeral. This had been their last chance to do something for their son, and gave them back that part of their role as parents.

Someone once asked me what was the worst kind of loss a person can suffer, and I could only say that no one type of death is worse than another. It all depends on the circumstances the bereaved are in at the time and how they accept the passing. However, I do feel drawn to try to help those who have no answers at all after a death, even to the extent of not knowing if their loved one is dead or alive.

A year or two ago I was asked to give a sitting to a family whose seventeen-year-old son had gone missing in Glasgow. He had disappeared on his first night out with his new colleagues at his first job. His mother had been wrestling with a growing sense that something terrible had happened, and the Scottish media had taken up the story. A couple of weeks had passed with no advances in the police investigation, and a friend who worked for the papers brought the family to me.

I had reservations about seeing them as I knew that if their son did indeed come through it could only confirm to them immediately that he was dead, and I'd be the one to deliver this devastating news. When his parents came to see me I asked them if they were really braced to hear the worst, as their weeks of alternating hopes and fears would be resolved in a very short time indeed. They all agreed that they had to know whatever there was to know; closure was the most important thing they needed.

I didn't even have to tune in – it was as though the boy was standing behind my shoulder, talking straight into my ear. He started to give me facts and personal details about his life that his family could understand, and I passed them on to the three sitting opposite me, watching them anxiously. It had to be personal as so much of the information about his case had been broadcast in the media that I needed to assure the parents that I was no con artist.

There was a moment when I noticed a look on his father's face which told me that he realized that if I was giving them this information, it must be coming from his son. Seconds later his sister registered the same thing, and lastly the mother. Then the boy told them that there was no foul play involved. He had fallen into the Clyde and drowned, and they would find his body in a particular place on the river bank in a few months time. When this happened, he said, his family would benefit more from what he had to say now as they would know it really had been him who was communicating. It would become more relevant, and they would really be able to heal themselves then with his help.

Months later, at the time the Spirit had predicted, I read in the local press that his body had indeed been found in exactly the place he had stated. His family could finally grieve and find total closure. They had known for some time that his Spirit still existed and that he was not in any pain or danger, and that there was nobody walking around the same streets as them who was responsible for his death.

At some point I will give the same family another sitting when they feel ready but I hope that their son's Spirit intervention has already made what they are going through a bit easier.

CHAPTER EIGHT

Jewels of the Mind

Jewels of the Mind

The psychiatrist Elizabeth Kübler-Ross wrote in her 1969 book, *On Death and Dying*, that those who have been given a terminal diagnosis go through five distinct stages of adjustment. First, denial, when they try to block out that such a thing is happening to them; then anger, as they ask why it is they who have been dealt the blow. Next they try to bargain, saying they'll be a better person if only they are saved. The penultimate phase is one of depression and simply not caring any more. The last is acceptance.

Since then it's been popular to look on these steps as a model for those left behind to deal with grief too, with some counsellors even insisting that the bereaved must work their way systematically through in the correct order. In years of work as a medium I have seen people handling the terrible pain of grief in all kinds of different ways, but I can't say that there is some kind of 'system' to guide you through.

All that matters is that you eventually accept the death of your loved one, and learn to live your life while celebrating theirs. It doesn't matter how you get there, or how long it takes, just so long as you are at peace with yourself and know that you will keep your bond with them, in this life and the next.

My goal as a medium is to help people break through to this acceptance, turn a corner in their sorrow and walk out the door to get on with their life. I'm not trying to encourage them to return again and again. Sometimes the Spirit has been trying to get through but the bereaved has effectively blocked them – I'm just giving the bereaved licence to open up and start to mend.

In 1995 I saw a man in his early thirties whose mother had passed the year before. He felt completely isolated and had spun into a depression; he could not think of his mother without feeling pure rage that she had deserted him, as he saw it. They had been each other's only family for much of his life as his father had left them years ago and not bothered to contact them since.

It was explained to me almost at once by the Spirit lady that she could not get through to her son because of this anger, even though she had tried to impress his mind and thoughts with certain memories in the hope of letting him know that she was still spiritually connected with him. She said something that sounded fairly trivial to me, that on Sundays in particular she tried to comfort him.

At this, though, the man collapsed and began to cry, saying that now he knew it was really her coming through to him. It turned out that although they shared the same house and saw each other daily, on Sundays they had always set aside the day to talk and catch up with what had happened that week over dinner. When she had passed he'd found that every coming Sunday laid him so low as he thought what he'd lost that he developed this fury against her for breaking their special bond.

The lady in the Spirit world explained that she'd tried to reach his mind many times but he was turning away her attempts, wanting more proof instead. He wanted to see her, rather than trusting his own thoughts, which were actually being impressed by her in person. When that didn't happen he thought of her as dead, and thoughts of his own death followed inevitably.

The upshot of the meeting was that the young man left me saying that each Sunday he would open his mind to his mother, firstly by remembering the good years they shared and the bond between them, and then by telling her about his week, quite like old times. The knowledge that she really was there made him feel immeasurably less lonely, and gave him something positive to focus on. Never mind those five stages of grief – the first phase for moving on with your life is to open up rather than shut down.

Some people deal with those stages even before their loved one has parted. They are well prepared for a particular death and if they do decide to consult a medium, they don't have many questions, but rather seek one quick clarification from a loved one. These sittings usually run very smoothly and are satisfying to everyone concerned.

One elderly lady who came to see me made a point of telling me outright that she wasn't sad to have lost her husband, but just needed to be sure that he was still in existence in Spirit. When I asked my Spirit guides if he was there, John came through very fast, giving his name and saying that he 'never got home'. The lady smiled warmly, and I knew we must have reached him.

He went on to explain that he had gone out one morning to buy a newspaper and collapsed and died in the street. John told her he had not felt a thing and that he knew she had coped well with his passing and was troubled only by the fact that she had not been with him when it happened. They had had, he said, a pact that they would be by each other's side and hold hands when the time came to go. They had also promised each other not to be sad, but to carry on living fully until they could be together on the other side once more.

He let her know that she must go on enjoying her life with their children and many grandchildren and look back on their own time together with pleasure. At this point the lady stopped the sitting, thanked me and smiled wisely. When she left I realized that the only reason she'd needed to get through to him was to have that one last moment with him that she had been denied because they were apart when he passed. She missed him, but she did not fight his passing, and the knowledge that they had had something so special in each other in life meant that she had been able to let go.

It would be daft to say that grief should be so easy for everyone, as people's circumstances are so different and deaths can be far, far crueller than their gentle experience had been, but there are ways you can ease your sorrow and take courage in the face of your loss.

When I was working in America recently a woman in the audience raised her hand during a question-and-answer session and asked me why she was still so haunted by her mother's death, nine years after it had happened. She said that every time she thought of her mother she remembered her death. Spontaneously I replied: 'Have you ever tried to remember her life?'

It's as though people believe that they must not revisit happier times in their mind because it will only make their grief more acute. They think only of what they are missing, and not of the joys they have *had* and experienced, and this leaves them with nothing to focus on but the saddest time when their loved one was parting. I would argue the opposite.

The memories we have stored up in our hearts will remind

us of life, not death, and are the key to the healing process. People who are experiencing loss need to understand that the instant when their loved one passed was brief compared to the mass of experiences the departed knew in life, and that they must never give death a disproportionate emotional weight. We have wonderful images and scenes that are ours to recall whenever we choose.

When the Spirits give evidence to prove their continued existence they also trigger recollections of private jokes, glorious holidays, weddings, births – instances when they were especially close to their loved ones. Instead of the mind being a prison in which cyclical, depressive thoughts lead back only to death and separation, it becomes a refuge.

I like to say that the human mind is like our own personal jewel box which we can open at any time to contemplate the precious memories. We must try to remember that they are there, and can be used as a tool to lift us when replayed and that there is no restriction on how many times we may choose to watch them. The jewel box where we store our life's events is the same place where we are truly connected to all whom we love and who love us and I don't for one minute believe that that place in us ever dies.

The jewels are there to share too, and by talking with others who knew our loved ones we can animate the life we have lost, and slowly begin to heal. I don't think mediums are here to wave a magic wand and mend the broken-hearted but I do think that by letting the life that comes after death speak through us, we can give people a chance to stop death overshadowing the life that comes *before* it too.

One of the most remarkable stories of this use of memory came from a private sitting which should have, by all accounts, been a bleak occasion. I was introduced to a lady called Linda and I was immediately struck by her quiet strength and dignity; she did not seem crippled by grief as is often the case with people who are referred to me.

As I tuned into the Spirit world I became immediately aware of a little boy's voice, and could see him laughing and jumping up and down exuberantly, like any child his age. His mother didn't weep when I told her, but smiled and said, 'That's my boy, Jason.' Jason was busy telling me that he had no hair because of his treatment and he brought up all kinds of details of the hats his mum had bought for him to wear. He'd loved American football, and she'd bought him lots of caps with the different team insignia on them. Then he burbled out the names of all the other children on his ward and those of some of the nurses who had looked after him.

It was lovely to pass on his happiness and enthusiasm to a sitter who was so at ease and prepared to accept that her little boy was safe on the other side. Each time I told her something new she would grin or laugh as though she was fully experiencing her son's Spirit. When I described how much the little boy loved to hug her, she wrapped her arms round the front of her body and hugged herself, reliving the feeling of it.

The session lasted an hour – a long time by anyone's standards – and I felt like the details passing back and forth between mother and son covered all kinds of areas of his short life. He reminded her of his favourite toys and games, and how he loved his dog, Max. There were memories of his family and his friends – it seemed like his time in this world had been rich and happy.

When we had finished, I asked Linda a few questions as I wanted to know more about these two remarkable people. She seemed surprised to have to explain that her son had had leukaemia, as I expect the way that I was relaying everything he said might have given her the impression that I somehow had the whole picture already.

He had died only eight months earlier, and I marvelled at her composure and the way she had come to terms with his death so swiftly. She considered the things I asked her and then began to talk to me at great length about this very special little person whom she said had brought hope to many people around him, even though he knew he would die for a year before he actually passed.

He'd snuck into the doctor's office one day and hidden behind a desk so he could jump out and frighten his mother when she was consulting the specialist about her boy's illness. He overheard her getting the awful prognosis, and stayed tucked away until she left the room. Two weeks after this he had announced to her that he knew he would die and asked her to promise him not to be as sad as she was when the doctor told her and she had broken down.

He said he had thought about it and he wanted his mum to laugh and have fun when they were together and not think about his illness. I tried to imagine what it could be like to have your six-year-old tell you something so destroying, but Jason was no ordinary child.

As the months went by he got inevitably sicker and was kept in hospital for longer and longer periods of time and the strain on Linda was starting to tell on her. One day she arrived at the ward to find one of the nurses sitting at her desk and weeping. When Linda asked what was wrong, the nurse said that she was not upset but had been moved by something Jason said to her.

A few minutes before, the nurse had seen Jason with a deep frown on his face and asked if he was all right. He told her that he was worried about his mother, because he had told her she should always be happy when they were together and that maybe if she wasn't allowed to be sad now she might always be sad after he died. He didn't want that to happen. The nurse was so moved by his compassion that she quickly made her way back to the nurses' station and cried.

When she heard this, Linda also welled up and let out huge sobs. She couldn't believe that her little boy could think like this and she told me that something in her had changed from that moment. She said that after that, every moment she could spend with her son she tried to be happy, but also honest about her feelings.

When his time came he told his mum that she was always to remember the funny moments and the laughs they had shared to keep herself happy. The surprising thing for Linda was that although this was a tall order, it seemed to be easy – every time she thought of Jason after he had gone, she found herself smiling and recalling the sound of his laughter. Then she would think of how tightly he would hold her when she arrived at his bedside or was about to leave.

Something she told me which I have passed on to many others who are grieving is this: 'When I remember my son in his short life, I know that he truly lived and that fact helped me when it was time to let him go. I feel so sorry for people who can only remember how their loved one died.'

Jason not only helped his mother, but she also told me that many of the nurses use examples of his bravery and spirit when dealing with other parents who are just about to go through a similar time with very sick children. Linda likes this as she feels that her son lives on through many people and his death may in some way heal the hearts and minds of others, as a story that can help to console them.

By sharing these memories of her son, Linda did not, of course, lose any of their potency – they still meant as much to her, if not more. If you share grief, however, and in particular with someone you are closest to, you may find that it is less of a burden as a result. There is a great difference between telling a professional counsellor or therapist about your darkest moments and being able to pour out your heart to a loved one who cares deeply about you in turn.

I was running a residential weekend in England in 2004 when a true example of this crossed my path. At the end of each evening we'd sit and swap tales in the small lounge of the hotel where we were staying. It was a nice way to round up the day's seminars and was pleasant and relaxing. Everyone had a reason to attend this course which involved mediumship and spiritual healing, and the exchange of life stories probably helped people learn more than they had in the lectures and classes.

There was a man called Mark who was in his late thirties and was attending with his partner James. They had only been together for two years and were having difficulties as Mark was undergoing episodes of deep depression. His former partner Ian had died five years earlier, and he was plagued by guilt. Mark and James had sought help because they knew what they had together was worth fighting for and were willing to exhaust every avenue to keep their relationship alive.

It was Mark who one night began to tell me that he had already grieved for Ian and that he was sure he was over it. He was adamant that it couldn't be that which was holding him back. He didn't mind telling me that he had hit the bottle heavily after his partner died and had attempted suicide several times before he began to accept his loss.

He'd lost all his friends and close family then too, as none of them could stand his behaviour. In the end, they'd all given up trying to help. He signed himself into a clinic and began the long, tough withdrawal from alcohol. He tried to sort through his thoughts and straighten out his mind, but it wasn't till he met James that he felt happiness start to unfurl inside himself once more for the first time since his loss.

Now, after two years with James, he couldn't understand how despite his great love for him, his joy was undercut by old sorrows. The wounds he thought he'd healed were reopening.

I didn't need to be a medium to see that while Mark had overcome his depression and alcoholism he had never truly handled the loss of Ian. He'd never allowed that guilt and anger any expression during his mourning and now they were swamping him and he didn't have the crutch of booze to help him. The whisky bottle had been good enough anaesthesia for a while until he staggered far enough to reach his next 'cure' – therapy – and then found James.

They were so euphorically happy that he let that emotion plaster over the problem, but now that they were over their honeymoon period, although they still adored each other, the reality of these old, undealt-with feelings was crowding in on him. He had never accepted the death, nor had he been able to share his fears about it with someone close.

Mark didn't see things this way, but confided in me that he thought the memories were coming back because Ian was upset that he was with a new partner, and was impressing negative thoughts on his mind to part him from James. It was astonishing to think that anyone would suspect a loved one in the Spirit world of this – they would never seek to rob us of happiness, especially after we had gone through the kind of traumas Mark had faced.

Time and again I've seen depressed people believing that the negativity they suffer comes from Spirit, and that's because they see nothing but bleakness in death, rather than a life after life. I wanted to interrupt, but I didn't. I let Mark continue his tale until he finished by telling me he was looking for a medium so that he could see if it was indeed true that Ian was furious with him and holding him back.

The thing was, that weekend Mark had approached me several times for a private sitting and each time I had felt that the time was not right. I thought he should help himself first, even if I could help him too. On that last night when we were talking, I asked Mark and James if they had found a message in the seminar. They both agreed that they had, and that they understood more about Mark's grief and had seen others who were attending who had worked through their sadness and started to move on because of their understanding of Spirit.

This all sounded promising, but I still couldn't shake off the impression that neither of them had grasped what was crippling Mark. I didn't tune into the other side to find Ian, but decided to try to explain to Mark how I saw things. I told them that I thought that now was truly the time for Mark to tackle his grief as he had a true partner in James whom he could trust to take everything he threw at him.

It was the security he felt with James that allowed Mark to be vulnerable by revisiting that terrible time after Ian died; he was strong enough to think of the future positively too. The guilt he felt was the kind of guilt so common to those left behind, the muddled 'Why-didn't-I?' and 'Why-couldn't-I?' thinking that has to be broken before it consumes everything.

I ended up by trying hard to convey to Mark that no-one was haunting him but himself, and Ian would never attack him or feel betrayed or envious. It wasn't that he couldn't love again, rather that the love he had with James gave him the space and confidence to face the terror of grief. I asked Mark to think of Ian and the love and joy they had once shared and to talk to James about it, so he could understand this part of his life and the trauma of losing him. If they could overcome that together they could also share the positive memories of Ian and celebrate them, and their own bond would be strengthened.

When the weekend was over we all went our separate ways, and Mark and James thanked me and said they'd think over what I'd said. I hope the two men found the answer they were looking for, even without intervention from Spirit. As much as we need to keep our link to those who have passed, we must never overlook what we have in this life too.

Though this life is the hardest we will face, we should never look on it as something to be merely endured until we can pass over into the Spirit world and be with our loved ones, as if we do so we might deprive ourselves of other joys that our departed friends would never want us to forego. This is the story of one woman called Marie whom I met at a Spiritualist church in Glasgow, who learned this lesson herself.

I didn't know her circumstances when I met her, but she had

that look so familiar to me of one who feels not just bereaved but as though a part of themselves has been removed. Her eyes were blank and she moved in a strange, methodical kind of way, as though it took an effort to go through the motions of everyday life. I later found out that she was recently widowed, after years of happy marriage to a man called Danny. He had not been ill for long, so his death had been quite a shock. She said that if I could not give her a reading she didn't want to continue in life and frankly didn't care if she died. She said a devastating thing: 'I don't think there's any life left in me any more.'

I wanted to help, so arranged a private meeting which I could tape for her, so she'd have something to take away from the session. When we met again it didn't take long for Danny to come through to her; as soon as I told her she sat bolt upright and looked for the first time like someone who was filled with Spirit. She focused intensely on me.

Danny gave me bits and pieces of evidence of their life together to convince her that it really was him, and conveyed some private comments that could only have come from him as far as Marie was concerned. She accepted these and I could see her visibly grow happier and happier – it was like watching a black-and-white photograph warm into colour. Danny also said that by thinking that their love had died with him, she was sapping her own will to live.

Marie agreed that this was what was causing her most distress. From his communication that day she drew some hope in the belief that their love was not destroyed by death, and Danny told her that she must look for that love in herself and in everything that was connected to their life together, in particular their family. When the sitting was over, Marie left with the tape recording and I waved her off, hoping that she would now have turned a corner in her grief.

However, not long after this sitting, I noticed Marie appearing at just about every public talk I gave in Scotland and even some of those I attended in England. She always fixed her eyes on me as though willing a message from her husband, but he was not one of the voices that spoke through me at any of those events.

When the talks were over she would push her way past everyone to speak to me and fix me again with that commanding look to try and force Danny to communicate, but I couldn't help as I could feel nothing from him in Spirit. Once I tried to remind her of Danny's message to look for their love in herself and make the reconnection that way. I suggested she listen to the tape again and go over what he had said. She didn't need me to feel close to Danny once more.

Several years passed, and one day when I was working in my barber's shop I spotted Marie walking by, and went out to have a chat and see how she was doing. She looked like a different woman, full of Spirit. We went for a coffee and she told me that after the last time we'd seen each other she'd gone home and listened to the tape over and over again until she finally understood what Danny had meant.

After that her world had been transformed – she'd started to notice Danny in so many things in her life, especially in their two children and everything they did. He was in the house and in the music they had enjoyed together. He was in the garden he had tended so carefully, and, more importantly by far, he was in her heart and mind. When she thanked God for the precious times they had had together it made her look at the whole situation in a different way. She stopped going to mediums and psychics and didn't return to the Spiritualist church which had been her second home when Danny passed.

I was delighted to see her so well, but when we'd finished our coffee I had to get back to the shop for a customer's appointment, and just as I was making my goodbyes she said, 'Wait, there's something else.' She then went on to tell me that one night, six months earlier, she'd felt an incredible urge to go back to the Spiritualist church. It was as though there was an important reason – Danny giving her a little push, almost.

After much deliberation she set off for church, filled with hope in case there was some new message from Danny.

The service progressed, but nothing came through from him. Marie felt a little let down by the gut feeling that had sent her out there that night. Making the best of it she made her way to the tea room to catch up with some of the old faces from her time there, when she was introduced to a fifty-something man whom she was told had lost his wife. His name was Keith.

Something clicked with Marie and Keith, and they chatted for some time. Marie felt the same 'gut feeling' that had brought her there and wondered about it. After that night she and Keith became good friends and started to see each other regularly and were indeed very happy. As she finished her story I reflected on the way that both had lost their life partner and lived through death and *despite it*, and that their faith in the afterlife had brought them together. By letting Spirit into their lives they had found a powerful friendship in this world.

For Marie, it was partly their garden that fostered her fond memories of Danny. When you are trying to progress in your grief, it sometimes helps to have a physical object like that which you can treat as a source of focus. It's common for people to surround themselves with the things that their loved ones owned in life, especially tokens like scarves or jewellery which have been worn so much they feel imbued with some of the essence of the one who has passed.

It's like there is a little piece of the life-force energy held forever in amber in our stuff or the homes and even places we have worked in or visited. I quite understand when I hear of a grieving person who wears a piece of their loved one's clothing or sits in their favourite chair. This is a natural instinct and stems from the animal instinct which is in every human being; it's raw and natural, yet because we don't often understand our behaviour in such actions, it makes us feel that we are doing something out of character.

It's an almost literal way of making a connection to the other side, and to the life you have shared at the same time. As long as we have something which holds a memory in its fabric, we have proof that our partner or child or friend lived, and by holding that possession we link to their mind in some way. It can also trigger a replay of the scenes and anecdotes you had with the loved one and that you still treasure – just the kind of healing memories we should seek out and embrace.

A photograph can recall a single instant frozen in time, but objects contain a story which travelled with the loved one through many different periods and events of their life. Many people have told me over the years that by wearing a ring or a watch of a lost relative they keep them in their hearts and minds, and it works as a kind of psychic key to open happier memories.

I know a lawyer, Robert Davies, who sought my help to reach his twenty-year-old daughter who had been killed in a skiing accident in the Alps. He wore her ring on his little finger throughout the sitting and every time I mentioned his girl he held the ring in his fingers as though it became charged with his daughter's life force. When he had flown out to France after her death to deal with the authorities he was given her possessions by the police and without thinking had immediately taken out the ring and slipped it onto his hand, and hadn't taken it off since.

I didn't need my Spirit guide to tell me that the ring was connected to someone he had lost and wanted to contact. It was obviously a woman's ring, and looked odd on his hand. His daughter came through strongly when we began the sitting. She told me her name and age and that she'd been at university at the time she died.

She gave some more personal clues to convince him finally that it was indeed she who was speaking and added that she was glad he was wearing the ring as he'd bought it for her for her fourteenth birthday. She was able to reassure him that she was neither lost nor alone in Spirit and that she wanted more than anything for her mother and father to be happy again. She said she would try to make them aware of her presence if she could.

Robert was a very thoughtful man with a lawyer's concentration and attention to detail. He listened intently to every word, and sometimes a tear or two welled up in his eyes; he'd nod or smile shyly to acknowledge what was said. Right the way through the hour we had together he held that ring tightly and I wondered if he believed that if he let go of the band for a second, the connection to his little girl on the other side would be broken.

When I began to lose the link to his daughter, Robert let go of the ring and looked down at his hand. I remember that I remarked to him that he felt her close when he held it, and he looked embarrassed. I told him it was ok to want her near and a good thing, as she herself had said, that he wore it. He'd always know the scene at her fourteenth birthday when he had given it to her, and think of all the things she'd done in life, living it to the full.

I have no idea if the ring was financially valuable; that certainly wasn't the point. Heirlooms like that come charged with the power to let us open the jewel box of memories we carry in our minds – and those are the true precious possessions.

Many mediums and psychics use these objects themselves to help them make a connection to Spirit, and the practice is called 'psychometry'. Those who work with the police to try and solve murder or missing persons cases in particular make use of this, tuning into the item. It would seem that we can leave lasting impressions of our character and important memories of our lives in things which we keep close to us and you needn't be a psychic to pick up on that.

As the object is solid it fortifies our memories, adding reality and grounding us at the same time. I often wonder when I'm walking down the street or sitting somewhere to watch the world go by, how many of the people who pass are wearing someone else's memories and how many times they have let that memory play out. I hope they can make the link beyond the object to the Spirit too.

Some folk can't see their loved one's things in the same way, and become almost scared of them. It's as though the trinkets take on a taboo status, as a source of harm, not comfort. People become scared that it would be too painful to hold something which was so recently close to their loved one. It's a fear of the physical side of death as well as a reluctance to return to memories of someone who will not come back in this world.

Speaking to the mother of a young soldier who was killed in the Gulf, I not only passed on the news of his survival, but also little tales from his life that his mother had been desperate to avoid thinking of in her grief. She was uplifted by what he had to say, and even long after he had ended the communication she was laughing as she cried, and telling me more things about what he'd got up to.

One thing above all that brought her relief was the way he told her that when she got home she must open up a cupboard where she'd locked away all his childhood things and take them out and look for more memories of his life. By shutting them away she was denying so much that was positive, and staving off her acceptance of his death. Now she could revel in the good times they had shared, just as he wished for her.

When we lose someone, one of the ways we can share their memory and help it live on is to tell stories about them, and objects can work like a box of props to illustrate that. Holding a photograph, we can explain to someone who never knew our loved one what happened on that day the picture was taken, and why it and the lost one were special. When we pass on a necklace to a granddaughter who never knew her grandmother we're recounting tales that will help a new generation to imagine and commemorate people who meant so much to us. They may never have been close in life, but the link through Spirit is enhanced and spelt out. To share an object is to share a memory.

It is, however, important not to make a fetish of the bracelet or the shirt or whatever it is you hold dear at the expense of the very real link to the other side and the memories in your 'jewel box'. Even if you lose this 'key', you can still open the door.

Alex Barker was a man whose wife had died young of breast cancer, and when he lost her wedding ring he was wracked by guilt. He'd worn it on a little chain around his neck after she passed and whenever he needed to think of her he only had to hold it and memories of their wedding day would come flooding back to him. When he realized the chain had snapped and the ring was missing, he thought the connection to his wife was gone forever and he would never revisit those happier times.

His wife knew better. During his sitting she convinced him that it was not the ring which magically held the memories, but his own mind. He left the session with his conscience eased and a renewed conviction that she was still there, watching over him and living on in his heart.

At around the same time I came across a woman whose mother had died some time ago and who had believed she was over the worst of her grief. However, she had mislaid a gold locket that her mother had always worn, and which contained a small picture of her mother and father when they were first married. She was plunged back into despair at this, tormented with the idea that her mother in Spirit must be furious as it had been her favourite item of jewellery.

Every time she thought of her mother she thought of the locket, and that just made things worse. It turned out that once again the Spirits had a different take on the situation, and her mother, who was not in the least upset, was able to reassure her and to tell her where the token was, to her great relief.

Another interesting observation I have made with bereavement is the difference between the way someone who has experienced their first loss behaves compared with another who has had many losses in their life. Those who are experiencing grief for the first time look like they are going through a maze in their own mind and seem desperate for answers. They fight their feelings and try to hold back the emotions which are waiting to overwhelm them. The nervous energy they emit could be cut with a knife.

Someone who has been through this before, on the other hand, seems to have a place to go to inside themselves, a place they have been before and know that they can draw on. Those who have been bereaved several times carry a weight which they have carried before and even though they feel the same pain, it is like a recurring illness. At first it caused them fear and distress, but with each bout they learned to live with its conditions and accepted the terms more calmly.

I remember first noticing this with my own mother. She's lost so many family members – her mother, her father, one of her own children, and in recent years every one of her sisters and brothers whom she'd raised almost as her own. She has always been a rock for those around her, and even in mourning she never gave up that role.

When the last of her brothers, John, was dying only three weeks after being diagnosed with leukaemia, we thought she might finally have had enough.

She said to me, 'I've got to go through this one more time. He's not coming out of hospital, is he?' I shook my head. 'Fine,' said my mum. 'Let's deal with it.' And she did. She and my father were like the A-Team – they set about preparing John's children, who had never experienced a death before. She sent me to break the news to his grandson, and I told him that his granddad was dying, and that if he wanted to go in and talk to him now, he'd remember that conversation for the rest of his life.

Mum went to John's son and daughter and when they said they were thinking of transferring him to a private hospital to be cured, she was very firm in telling them that it would do no good. She swung into action, helping them deal with all the practicalities of a death. She knew they wanted his funeral to be a good send-off, so she helped them find all his favourite music and organise a spread of his favourite food for the wake.

When it came, the funeral was especially hard for her, as John was the first person in the family to be buried with her mother back in Glasgow. I asked my mum if she wanted to go up to the grave's edge, and she said, 'No, it's sixty years since I stood at that graveside, burying my mother, and John was thirteen and he threw himself into that grave after her. I was nineteen. I had to drag him out. I don't have to go up there and feel that again.'

It was the same look I saw in my mother's eyes that day that I have seen so many times with those who have lost an entire family. The same behaviour too, which is like resignation to the reality of death combined with the ability to move on to the next episode of life – not because you want to, but because you have learned with experience that you have to do just that. I do believe that we all possess the ability to cope with loss in our life and as much as I feel that I have an ability to help some people at such times, there are people, like my mother and many, many others, who go within and find a strength of their own inner Spirit to drag them through their grief.

My cousins were amazed at her too, and one of them said to me, 'She's so hard! Doesn't she feel anything?' and I could only reply, 'You have no idea.' I thought it could be strength, but now I think it's courage, and also a learned behaviour – an instinct for self- preservation, even – and I know she's one of the bravest people I've ever seen in the face of death.

CHAPTER NINE

Healing Life and Death

Healing Life and Death

I've written about my early psychic experiences in *Spirit Messenger* and *The Unbelievable Truth*, and how I was unable to grasp what was happening when I saw people I should not have seen, or had premonitions of things that were coming in the future. If I told any grown-ups they were always unnerved, so I learned to keep the visitations and funny ideas to myself. They never scared me, but the reaction of adults did. The Spirit phenomena left me feeling dreamy, with a sense of complete internal stillness, as though I was surrounded by a force that held me in a comforting way.

These experiences became less and less frequent as I grew up and by my late teens they had stopped altogether. It wasn't until my early twenties that they started up again, and I saw Brian, the brother of one of my best friends, standing at the foot of my bed. He had been killed in a house fire that very night.

The experience brought the memory of my other 'spooky' happenings flooding back and I decided that I should investigate this side of my personality. I started to attend a Spiritualist church, discovering a religion that centred on demonstrations of mediumship, spiritual healing and other psychic phenomena. There were plenty of people with clairvoyant and other such gifts, and the people in the congregation accepted the messages that came from them as coming from the other side.

I went to the services for several months, and many times the mediums who were working would single me out and tell me I was a natural medium myself. They advised me to hone my gift, and, curious, I did just that. I joined a development class under the guidance of my teacher, Mrs Primrose. Before I started being taught systematically, most of my communication with the Spirit world was very one-sided and tended to happen *to* me, as I had little control over what was going on. I didn't know how to respond or what to do about it.

Mrs P was the best teacher I could have wished for; she was a tiny little woman but she could make a grown man cower. She could roar like William Wallace! She was a very spiritual person too, and that just gave her even more authority. She was a real gatekeeper to the knowledge of the Spirit world, because she wouldn't stand for any nonsense. Nothing got past that woman! She stopped me in my tracks when I was trying a bit too hard to be what I thought a medium should be: she'd just tell me to pack it in and be myself instead. She was absolutely right – you can't put on airs and graces or affect all sorts of mannerisms and still be a good medium.

I learned how to meditate and realized that the state of calm I'd felt as a child in my Spirit encounters was in fact the sort of mind-set you should aim to have so that the Spirit can enter. I began to understand that no medium could conjure up the Spirits at will and make them communicate. Contact could only happen when the Spirit wished it, or felt that the time was right. I now knew that my unpredictable Spirit messages as a child had occurred because the Spirits knew that someone was in a dicey emotional state and was trying to reach them, via me. I was just the go-between, a mediator to deliver a message, much like a telephone.

The development group gave me the time and space to test the Spirits and build up a trust which I insisted had to prove to me beyond doubt that all the information I was being given was from an intelligent source whose intention was to help people. If I was going to be the messenger, I wanted the message to be accurate! In seven years under Mrs Primrose's expert eye I found my own Spirit guides and learned to interpret the sensations by which they might introduce themselves to me.

When I started out I thought that a Spirit would just come and talk very clearly in my ear, and show me things. I also worried that nothing would come through, and it would be my fault; I cared a lot about what other people would think of my attempts at mediumship. I didn't want to get things wrong in public. In time I got to see that my gift worked better if I let go of these fears and just let my Spirit guides dictate to me.

Others may take strange interventions or mysterious happenings in their lives as divine guidance or something angelic – or just coincidence – but I discovered that *everybody*, not just mediums, has a higher form of guidance in a spiritual sense, which may or may not be able to make contact with them during their life on this earth.

It's essential for you as a medium to know that you are being guided and protected when you open up to the other world. The sense of safety I felt when I was first aware of my Spirit guides filled me with amazement. It's uplifting just to know that someone of a much higher nature is looking after you – or in my case, trying to, because I never thought I needed any assistance, thank you. I did need help though, of course.

The mistakes you make when exploring your gift of medium-ship are crucial to you as you progress – that's how you learn. You have to respect your Spirit mentors and understand that good will only come of using your skill if you let the guide impress details on your mind, rather than rushing in headfirst and making it up yourself unintentionally.

The process of trust started when I realized that my guide was setting me tests. I would be given information to research, and when I uncovered it this information would turn out to be very exact. I'd be shown visions of people or places, and then a day or two later I'd find the self-same person being introduced to me, or I'd wind up in a street or a room that gave me a jolt of déjà-vu.

I spent a lot of time meditating, and one night I was deep in thought when my guide impressed an image of Albert Best and myself working together in a large Spiritualist church packed with people. I was also given the image of a Tibetan deity and was told I would see this deity when I met Albert. I hadn't come across Albert at this stage, though I knew him by his reputation. As for the Tibetan image, that was all gobbledegook to me.

Two weeks later I was asked by the secretary of the Glasgow Association of Spiritualists if I would share a platform with Albert Best as the other medium they'd booked had dropped out. It was a fundraising night for a local charity. I agreed to take part and was thrilled to meet Albert. And, lo and behold, at the end of the evening he asked me for a lift home, as it was on my route. When we got back to his flat he invited me in and showed me a Tibetan Thanka painting – a sacred icon. The deity in the middle of it was the same one I had been shown by my guide just a fortnight earlier.

Inspired, I tried a new tack with my Spirit guides, and began to set tasks for *them*. I'd ask for information about a person I knew nothing about and no sooner would I send out that thought than details would come flowing into my mind. I'd then check this out and verify it for myself. Once I asked my guide to tell me about Mrs Primrose's husband, Robert, who had died some years earlier and whom I had never met nor heard much about.

The sequence that was impressed on me was of a man dropping dead in the street outside one of the Glasgow libraries, and Mrs Primrose kneeling down and desperately trying to help him. Even though something told me she knew he had passed, she stayed waiting for help, and eventually an ambulance came and took the body away. Mrs Primrose still stood in the street, but I could see the Spirit of the man standing beside her. Then the vision closed.

The next time I saw Mrs P I gently told her about the images I'd seen and she confirmed for me that was exactly what had happened when her husband died. She didn't mind the fact that I had been told these things, but was impressed at how accurately my guides had relayed the message to me.

The more I tested my guides, the stronger and stronger the answers became, and the bond between me and the guides was fortified. I understood what they wanted when I began to take on more and more jobs as a medium. They are my first points of contact, and if I don't feel their presence I can't continue. Spirits who want to contact a loved one through me have to come via the guides, who are the real conduits. I'm not the one who does the 'dialling'! Their aid is invaluable. Without some sort of spiritual guidance, mediums can become a law unto themselves and damaging to those who have come to them to seek assistance.

There are things that I don't totally understand about my guides, though – even whether I have many or it's just one who carries out different roles at different times. Guides seem to specialise – some are best with people who need a wake-up call from the Spirit world, others with those who have died violent deaths, still others with children. It's like having a specialist doctor for every kind of ailment. One of mine was a healer in life, and he is the guide who is there when I am working on a healing, not surprisingly.

If I am having difficulty understanding a symbol that is being shown to me, the guides will step in and that's when my mediumship works best. I'm not in a trance but my mind goes blank and the Spirit guides talk pretty much directly through me. I can't really say how they interact with the Spirits themselves, as that all happens behind the scenes as far as I'm concerned.

There are times when it seems like there's a system of messages lined up which must come through on one occasion – as though the Spirits were all in a queue, waiting for a chance to speak to their loved ones. I try not to tune into the other side before an open demonstration of mediumship has begun, because what tends to happen is that I 'download' the first message before I've even got to the audience. If I'm overtired, though, sometimes I can't help it and the spiritual script starts feeding into my conscious mind. It's also meant that I've sometimes received messages for people before they've even walked in the door!

You have to remember that the Spirits have often been working for a long while to bring people to a certain medium at a certain time, through synchronicity and impressing themselves on their loved ones' minds. It's their way of reaching them, and it means those messages are ready and waiting for delivery.

There was a superb medium working in the sixties who was a brilliant 'transmitter' of messages from the other side, but friends of mine who had readings with her have told me that was all she was willing to do – after she'd delivered the message she didn't want to give any of what you might call 'aftercare'. She just didn't want to go there with them.

Mediumship shouldn't be just that, though, and I think the healing and teaching side are totally essential. People always ask the same questions after a reading, and they need a medium to answer them. Things like, 'Where is my father now, if he can still talk to us?' and, 'What's happening to him? How can you tell this?' Not only do they have to go away and process all that, but they've got to explain it to family and friends too. That's why I think a medium has to make themselves as available to answer those sorts of questions as to give the evidence in the first place.

The human Spirit lives on after the loss of the physical body and the way it learns and grows from every experience means that it is indestructible. If there's anything that I could say has helped me to understand the nature of the human Spirit in this life or in the hereafter, it's this remarkable way it renews itself after every knock. I've come across people who have been dealt some of the worst blows that anyone could be expected to endure, but have shown amazing resilience and indeed become much stronger because of those trials.

When you look at the Spirit as being divine and out of the reach of human conflict, heartache and illness, you are immediately filled with a hope that whatever befalls you in this lifetime, you will be capable of dealing with it. Many who find themselves hit by tragedy or are hurt in a cruel way by another's inhumanity toward them may experience an instant separation from their divine source, leaving them to feel 'spiritless' and engulfed in loneliness.

It's in this loneliness that we experience the worst cancer known to man, and that is fear. I have found in my work that fear is what hurts most bereaved people in this world and stops them moving through their grief. That fear of separation, the fear that they have been cut off from someone they love and may never feel their loving presence again. I know that fear like this is only human and does not exist in the afterlife.

The same loneliness and fear are felt by people who lose a life partner through divorce and by those who have lost their direction in life unexpectedly. Some people have described experiencing the same feelings to me when they had been physically hurt, raped or abused. I see my job as helping people who are in this state of fear by reconnecting them to Spirit. If someone believes that I've given them a message from their lost loved one, then they can come to understand that they too are part of Spirit, and that opens up a whole new dimension to their life.

A half-hour sitting might be the starting point for a lifetime of soul-searching, but the most rewarding cases I've helped with have been those who went on from the session determined to look for more answers.

Nearly ten years ago I met a woman who had lost her son to suicide, and who got a beautiful message from him which helped her pull herself through the bleakest days of her life. It also led her to explore her own spiritual side, by attending lectures and seminars and reading plenty of books. She never overdid things, or became some kind of spiritual junkie in order to try to fill the void left by her son's death, but she arrived in her own way, very quietly, at a new way of thinking.

Now she has her boy in a part of her mind where she can go when she feels the need; sometimes she feels his presence and can just say, 'Hi, darling, how are you?' She doesn't need to speak to him mentally all day and every day. If she were the only case I'd helped with in twenty years I'd feel that I'd done a good job, just to see the progression she has made in her life.

The discipline of meditation over the years helped me to learn many things, not only about mediumship, but also about myself and how my mind worked. In order to be the best transmitter of messages I could be, I needed to be able to empty my mind and give the Spirits space – bandwidth, if you like. In order to do this I had to rummage around the mental garbage I'd gathered and discard a skipful. Maybe 'resolve' is a better word than 'discard' – the idea was that I could deal with a particular episode once and for all and put it to one side.

During my early meditations, I would find that as I tried to concentrate on something pure and spiritual, my thoughts would be guided to what felt like little dark rooms in the deepest departments of my mind. Memories would come out at me, which I had long forgotten or maybe hidden so deep that at first I never recognized myself in them or related them to my life.

If I didn't make peace with them, I'd find that whenever I settled down to meditate, one of these memories would emerge and replay itself, and, as if under hypnosis, I'd watch from a distance as I reacted to the experience all over again. It was extraordinary to see my old emotions from what felt like an out-of-body state and be able to analyse them without feeling affected by them. When I looked at some of these replays from my life, I wondered how I could have forgotten them or why I hadn't ever looked at them or tried to deal with them before. Once I'd sifted through the memories they were sort of shelved; I didn't worry about them any more, and more mental space was freed up for the Spirits.

I had to strip myself of pride and ego and open up to myself and recognize my flaws; once this warts-and-all soul-searching was complete I had to accept these faults and finally have compassion for myself as I was pieced back together again. The more truthful I was about myself, the more open I became and the clearer my mind was. This may sound pretty painful, but it was a journey that lightened my emotional baggage and let me take on life as it was, without deluding myself again.

Spiritual growth is a process not unlike bereavement, in that a part of you dies and you must progress despite that, which is exactly what the lady who lost her son to suicide discovered. You will hit low points and have to walk through the darkest nights of your soul before you can begin to recover. I still meditate every other day to be sure that I continue to keep my mind clear so I can be a good medium, and use my gift to help others.

There was one event from my childhood that surfaced during my years in development class, and which astonished me. In the memory I was about seven years old and at first I didn't even recognize myself. I was playing alone in the lane which connected to our back garden when I saw a man coming toward me. He was smiling at me but I could sense there was something very wrong about him. I didn't try to run away, though, but just froze and watched him get closer to me.

As the memory was playing out I had an overwhelming urge to back out of the memory and stop it before it ran its course. I wanted to open my eyes and come out of my meditation but something made me stay to watch. I could see the man putting out his hand to me, taking my arm and pulling me down into the long grass. I watched the child being abused.

From where I was, far in the future, I could do nothing to help the child. I remembered that when it had actually occurred I had just switched off mentally and never felt or did anything. As far as I was concerned as a child, it never happened and the entire scene was locked away deep inside my mind.

As an adult, though, I had to recognize that it had all taken place. I had to accept that too, and take it out into the open and let it go.

When I emerged from the meditation it was clear to me, as it hadn't been before, that I had done nothing wrong as a child.

Before that meditation all I had been able to remember of the incident was the man telling me that I mustn't tell anyone, and that it was our secret. He'd said that people would get hurt if I told someone, and I'd cause lots of trouble. I'm sure that's why the seven-year-old me tried to hide that memory away, hoping no-one would ever discover it and that it would die in that dark place. The mind is like the sea, though, and it gives up its dead eventually, and so I found the memory at a time when I was looking to find myself.

Afterwards there was nothing traumatic about recalling that episode; and I found it didn't affect me. I did wonder why I hadn't screamed for help, or told an adult about it, and I suppose it was because I thought no-one would believe me. What I did discover was that what was done was done, and that I shouldn't waste energy on something I couldn't change.

If I relived that moment every day and every hour, desperately trying to find a different resolution or to protect that child, I would only be trapped in it. The obsession would become consuming and would fill my thoughts with fear and hatred. By confronting what I had stowed away I made room for the positive, and found a source of inner strength.

It all came back to haunt me recently, though, which just goes to show how many levels of mind we have, and how far a memory can travel at the slightest trigger. Last year I found myself surrounded by a group of people who were pressuring me to keep certain things secret. None of them was being honest or open. The experience pitched me straight back to being that seven-year-old child who was told not to tell anyone what was going on, and to feeling completely helpless again.

Healing comes only from facing up to something like that, then moving on. If you don't, it'll resurface later and the memory will grow into an emotional re-experience of the situation – you'll find yourself living through everything you didn't allow yourself to feel at the time, whether you can control it or not. What is hidden is the thing that will haunt you, but when you can square with it and send it away, you are putting a light on in the dark. My meditation helped me to avoid this, because I re-experienced it while I was in that dreamy, meditative state.

Strangely, that feeling of dislocation that I experienced during the abuse was not unlike the trance-like state I use when I am reaching out to the other side, and I've toyed with the idea that this was the first time I actually encountered a state of connection to the Spirit world. It's common for people who have been in shock to have no proper, defined recall of that instant, and to talk of a sort of out-of-body experience that left them at peace. There are also many instances of folk who have developed psychic gifts after such an episode.

In America, the medium John Holland had a serious car accident when he was in his twenties, and tells me that when he was recuperating he couldn't remember the details of the crash, though he had been conscious throughout, but he had noticed the beginnings of his now fully-developed psychic ability. One of the best mediums of the Second World War, Helen Hughes, would tell people that she first knew she was psychic when she survived a near-fatal illness as a child.

As a healer or medium you could say that you need to have endured some kind of mental or physical trauma in order to be able to help others. You can help others to the extent that you have been hurt yourself. Let me explain. Your higher mind is the tool you need to work with the sitter, but you also operate on another deeper level – the one where your emotions from that terrible experience are stored, and that means that you know exactly what kind of a place the bereaved person opposite you has found themselves in. You can, in one sense, go down to meet them.

For many who end up working as a medium or healer, they were going through some kind of emotional turmoil at the time they set out on the spiritual journey. I wouldn't say you can't be a medium or healer without that, but it does give you an extra capacity for empathy. They're often people who have been taken to a very crucial point in their lives – like an illness, or a loss, or a relationship that had broken down – and from that they have come out of their darkest time with themselves with renewed energy and their new spiritual gift intact, and this has actually heightened their sensitivity.

After going through something terrible, you have the option to shut yourself down and avoid those who are also suffering, or to turn what happened to you into a force for good, using it to help others.

What meditation allows you to do is to use that experience without letting it overwhelm you. As a medium I have to use the distancing effect that meditation provides; not only to contact the Spirit world but also to avoid taking on the emotional suffering of those who come for sittings. I cannot afford to take on that suffering if I am to try to lift their mind out of heavy depressions and grief; my higher mind has to remain uninvolved and clear for the Spirits to communicate through. What good would I be to anyone if I cried or went all gushy every time I heard of someone's loss? A medium can't be pulled down into the emotional whirlpool of the sitter's mind.

I once met an extraordinary lady when I was travelling on the overnight train from London to Glasgow. We got chatting in the smoking carriage for no particular reason, and it was one of those strange, intense conversations that you can sometimes have with a perfect stranger because you know you will never meet again. Nothing prepares you for it, so every word is spontaneous and from the heart. I'm sure synchronicity has something to do with it too, and that your Spirit has somehow on some level choreographed the whole event.

The lady was in her fifties and very dowdy-looking with straggly brown hair, worn jeans and a baggy shirt. She was carrying a rucksack over her shoulder. When she entered the compartment she looked around for somewhere to sit, before settling on the empty seat opposite me. She didn't even ask if the seat was taken but pulled off her bag, sat down and immediately began to tell me about her day. She had a very strong but kind tone to her voice and I warmed to her straightaway as she told me about where she was going and what she was hoping to achieve in a tour around Scotland.

A short time into our eleven-hour journey, we were sharing opinions on life and solving the world's problems with the help of Scotch whisky and Benson & Hedges. It was around this time that we somehow got onto the subject of overcoming some of the biggest problems in our lives and how we both shared the similar idea, that everything in life is put before us for a reason. As I looked across the table at this strange lady I could sense that she was about to open up and reveal something in her life which would hold a deep meaning for me. I could tell by the change of note in her voice as she spoke more quietly and deliberately that she was now speaking from her soul and was beginning to release something from the very depth of herself.

She told me that when she was a teenager she'd spent a summer travelling around Europe with some friends. She met an older man in a bar in a French town where she was staying in a youth hostel. She said that she had felt very drawn to this man and that he became very affectionate toward her and was so polite and courteous she'd agreed to meet him the following day. Her friends were all very excited for her and encouraged her, telling her to go for it and have some fun. All in all, everyone felt that she would be safe and those of her friends who had met this man thought him nice, 'for an older guy'.

The next evening they met in a café not too far from where she was staying. She assured me that the evening was great and she thought her date was nothing more than charming when he asked her if she would like to see his apartment and have a coffee before he drove her home. She thought she had nothing to fear as she reckoned she was old enough to know what she was doing, and besides, he was kind and gentle to a fault. Somehow I knew what was coming in the story at this point, and I was dying to ask her a question, but she kept on talking, steadily, and I didn't dare interrupt. As they climbed the stairs to his apartment she felt a surge of fear run through her body and she stopped rigid for a moment.

Her companion sensed this and put his arm around her and

smiled, telling her it was ok and if she didn't want to go in he would take her home at once. She relaxed and followed him inside where to her horror she was faced with an empty room, with nothing but bare floorboards and blinds that were drawn.

She described to me in the train her feeling of hopelessness as she heard the key turn in the lock in the door behind her and two other men walk out from an adjoining room. Her description of what happened to her in that room gripped me with shock and complete terror; she just calmly told me how these three men had proceeded to rape her in turn. She must have caught the look on my face because she smiled and said something which I never expected to hear.

She said that although all of what she described to me sounded horrendous, nothing of this vile experience touched her soul. During the assault her mind had closed up, and sent her into a kind of dream state which is all she remembers when she tries to think over what happened. She can recall with clarity her fear on entering the flat, and how she felt when it was over and she came to and had to race for the door, pulling up her jeans as she went.

She hadn't gone to the authorities as she'd felt that she wouldn't be believed. Instead, this remarkable woman had promised herself that she would never let herself get into such danger again, and that she would keep thinking that she had at least come out of it all alive. I asked her, astonished, if she didn't despise those men for doing what they had done to her, and she only shook her head and said that every time she had tried to hate them she had found herself trapped back in that room.

I already thought this woman was pretty remarkable, but then she surprised me again. Lighting another cigarette, she quietly asked me if I had been through something similar. For a second the thought flashed across my mind that I wanted to say no, but before I could stop myself I said yes instead. She asked me if I wanted to talk about it and before I knew what I was doing, I was telling this stranger something I'd never told anyone else before – the story of being abused when I was seven.

As she'd found with her experience in France, I also had no real recollection of much of what had gone on, and just like her I had no real reason in my mind to feel hate for that man as he meant nothing to me now, years later. Like her I'd fought to turn the experience into something positive, that I could learn from; I'd also thought no-one would believe me if I went for help.

The parallels were amazing and we felt like we were comparing notes. The dream-like, disconnected state that took over when we were being attacked was exactly the same. In my talk with that lady I realized that the main thing to understand is that this detachment tells us that whatever terrible things are happening to our body, our *Spirit* is still intact. As the train rattled on, my companion and I agreed that if you comprehend that, then you know that you can and will survive any of the worst times that life can throw at you, and that even the trauma of death itself cannot destroy our most essential core.

The Spirit within us is our life-force energy in this world and it's what connects us to the Spirit world too. It talks to us all the time if we will hear it, and we're at our best when we move with the Spirit and follow its intentions. Many times I've witnessed people who feel no connection to their higher nature and think they are lacking in Spirit because they feel cheated or discouraged by events in their life. They get caught in inner grief and pain.

Both the lady on the train and I realized that we can heal our own lives from within ourselves and recognized that suffering and pain are part of our spiritual growth in this world. It didn't surprise me at all to learn that this lady was now a healer, as of course she wanted to help others who were wrestling with unimaginable horrors.

Five hours in that train passed like five minutes, and we were out of cigarettes. The conversation had become so profound so quickly that we hadn't bothered with the niceties of asking each other's name, and now that it was over we simply said goodnight and went off to our sleeping compartments, both with a kind of understanding that, spiritually, we had made a true connection.

CHAPTER TEN

First Contact

First Contact

Every medium's experience of Spirit communication is different, but the best description I've managed is that I'm using a kind of emotional telepathy which works in my mind when I am connected to Spirit. The first thing I am aware of is a sort of atmosphere or vibration – as though someone is shaking me from the inside and the movement is reverberating through me and out of me. That's what lets me know that the Spirits are near.

Once I sense that, I automatically think a question: 'Who is there?' The response is sometimes a mental image or a sound or voice – not generated by my own brain, but playing through it, and I begin to build a communication with the Spirit wishing to come forward. If I hear a voice in my head or close to my ear I know that I have a good communicator with me and I can ask questions directly to them. They then impress me with images of their lives. Sometimes I get a particular physical feeling which will tell me how the person died – a pressure on my chest if it's a heart condition, for example.

It's not a pain that harms me personally, nor do I even get

affected badly when I sense that the Spirit passed in a violent manner – a car accident, say, or murder. This sort of memory touches my mind and runs through my body but doesn't stay with me after the session or for any longer than it takes for me to describe it to the sitter. The Spirit world never wishes to harm us; they just want to get our attention.

As the sitting progresses I constantly ask the Spirit things mentally; I want to know as much as possible about them before I pass on the message they have for their loved one. I need to get evidence to the person sitting opposite me that the person tuning in is indeed their much-missed friend or relative. Sometimes the whole thing takes only minutes; sometimes it takes me longer to make a link, or the message is a particularly long and involved one. The joy which fills me when the link is made comes, I'm sure, from the feeling of reconnection between two souls whose minds have joined again and who know for certain that death has not severed their bond of love.

Before I go to work as a medium, I specifically try to lift my mind to the happiest thoughts I can conjure up, and I know a lot of other mediums who work the same way. I'm more likely to listen to the fastest, happiest, bounciest music I can find than to go to a quiet corner and meditate. You need to be literally in high spirits because you are going into a very dark place in people's minds.

As a medium you function as a sort of pulse transmitting that vibration from Spirit, and it's a pulse that ticks away far faster than the slow, depressed rhythm coming from the bereaved. It's like two different metronomes, one racing, one tocking at a fraction of the pace. At the same time my own level is being raised to meet that of the Spirit world, which operates at a higher level still.

That's how my mind feels when I'm working – like a constant, quick ticking-over and what I'm trying to do is bring the speed of the bereaved's vibration up to something more normal. I need to pick up their tempo and bring them back to real life – back to their heart rate, the true speed of life.

Grief slows down the human mind and forces it to turn in on itself and face grim realities. That's why we clutter our minds up with music and TV, to avoid thinking such things over. When we lose someone we're knocked out of that cluttered comfort and into those starker thoughts, and it's hard work. If you ask anyone who is intensely depressed how long a day is, they'll tell you it is endless – that's what I mean when I say that sadness slows you down. You are no longer running on the same frequency as the everyday. There are no distractions from a pain that has to be relived again and again.

If you strip away all the words and messages, what happens in essence is that I'm trying to leave the people who have come to see me with more 'oomph' and energy, to the point where they can go away feeling excited and alive. A medium can't cure everything but I do hope to help people function at a normal level and get on with life. I also consult a higher part of my mind – that which is in touch with the Spirit world – and ask it to bring the rest of my mind up to that level.

If my sitters leave feeling elevated and with the new ability to take an interest in the details of day-to-day life, instead of focusing on all the horrors and fears of a bereavement, I know I've done my job well. I take them away from the unnecessary, long-drawn-out thoughts; that to me is the mechanics of mediumship. They may not describe it in the same terms, and they may not understand how it happened, but they know they've undergone a change and can engage with the outside world once more. Some folk will slip right back out of that a short time after the sitting, but usually that spiritual boost is enough to kick-start most people again.

Sometimes in a sitting the interchange of these life rhythms just doesn't work. It might be that the sitter is not ready to recover yet, or that they have become so sunk in grief that they find it easier not to fight it. Usually I pick this up very fast – it's how I know if a sitting won't work. If there is no response from them I find myself dropping back down to the everyday rhythm, and increasingly drained of energy. There's a point at which, for the sake of my mind, I have to let them go as I can't mentally drag them up too far. They need to build their own momentum and meet me halfway.

In a good sitting I keep my 'line' open for as long as I can, as more than one Spirit may wish to come through to communicate with their relative on earth, but once the energy required to keep that line clear has faded, I have to end the session. It is not my physical energy so much as that of the Spirits on the other side that does this.

I have to be careful not to overstretch myself and try to do too much. To this end, I try to work as a medium during the times I've set aside for the Spirit world. It's very important that there should be an appropriate time and a place for the discipline, and that mediums don't whiz around leaving half a message here and half a message there. There have, however, been times when the Spirit world would set up a situation where I found myself directed somehow to someone who truly needed a message from their loved ones in the other world

On many occasions I've had an impression from someone in Spirit that I should head to a particular Spiritualist church, even though I have no appointment there and have never set foot in the place. It starts as a thought, then I begin to *know* that I should go there. If I fight it I get a rising sense of urgency which is impossible to resist. On almost all of these occasions I have followed the impulse, always to discover that the medium who was scheduled to be at the church had cancelled or was late.

You don't need to be at a church for the Spirits to reach you, either. I've had messages for people on trains, buses, and once even on a small jet plane. I'd been asked by a friend if I would like to share her trip from London to Glasgow in a private plane, and leapt at the chance. I thought it'd be great fun; who'd turn down a trip like that? As we were cruising along somewhere over the Midlands, the pilot nipped back to invite us to have a tour of the cockpit, which we accepted happily.

Once we got to the front of the plane and were being shown which of the vast expanse of winking lights and buttons did what, I suddenly had a very strong sense of a woman who had recently gone over into the Spirit world and wanted to talk to the co-pilot. She said this was her son. She told me her name and how and when she had died and I found myself telling the co-pilot, who was gobsmacked. Not what you want when you're tens of thousands of feet in the air, but there was no arguing with this Spirit. I passed more information along to him as quickly as I could, and the co-pilot didn't seem to be able to pay much attention to the controls any more. He made a sign to the pilot who came forward to take over and we retired to the cabin so I could finish the impromptu sitting.

The co-pilot confided to me that since his mother had died

six months ago he had been tempted to go to a medium, but hadn't known how to go about it. Well, his mother had obviously sorted it out for him!

That kind of spontaneous mediumship does, however, have to be an impulse that comes from Spirit, or else the whole thing gets gimmicky. There is nothing worse for a medium than to be asked to perform on the spot, but people who don't believe like to ask for a quick display to convince them. I can't begin to tell you how many times I've been asked to 'prove it', as if mediumship is a party trick. This sort of thing usually occurs during interviews with newspaper journalists or on radio or live television.

I'm very reluctant to get dragged into this sort of situation and deliver what I'd call a two minute 'McMessage'. It's silly to think you can give someone adequate evidence of their loved one's existence on the other side in one hundred and twenty seconds flat, and it certainly won't give them the profound spiritual exhilaration that should come from a good, detailed reading. It can work, but, to my mind, for all the wrong reasons.

I travelled to South Africa recently to promote one of my books. The flight was long and when I got off the plane I was looking forward to having a day to rest and acclimatize before the publicity tour began. My publisher greeted me with news that they'd been asked if I could take part in a TV talk show which was going out live the same day. I agreed, but only if I could unpack and refresh myself quickly beforehand. I had a gut feeling that the informal chat in the studio would turn out to be something different altogether.

The programme was called *Noeleen* after its host, a charming lady who was very interested in the subject of life after death and appreciated how tired I was after the ten-hour flight. I don't know if it was jet lag or the fact that I knew that the programme would be transmitted only in South Africa, but I abandoned my principles about McMessages when, one minute in, Noeleen asked for a demo.

I launched straight into a McMessage from Noeleen's grandmother in the Spirit world, rattling off bits and bobs of evidence like a horseracing commentator. When I paused for breath and caught Noeleen's eye, I saw that her jaw had dropped and there were producers hopping around behind the cameras calling for us to go to a break. The cameras switched off but I carried on, and by the time the adverts were over and we were live, the switchboards had lit up like the Blackpool illuminations. Everyone wanted to get in touch with someone on the other side.

I really don't know what happened to my boundaries that day, but I even started to get messages for the caller following the one I was talking to, before I'd even heard their names.

Overtired and overloaded with all the African Spirits who were desperate to come through, I couldn't stop until they closed the phone lines and ran the credits. I tried to explain to the studio audience that this was not how my gift was supposed to work and that in order to give a better, more uplifting message I needed to see someone privately or at a Spiritualist demonstration, where I could get a proper connection and really help them.

After that programme, wherever I went in South Africa people would come up to me and ask for a McMessage. It took a lot of explanation to convince them that this was not how I normally conducted myself. It might seem clever to knock out a McMessage to prove that the other side can reach us, but it in no way represents all of what can be done in the way of truly helping people who are deeply hurt by loss.

I've talked about synchronicity and the importance of following a gut instinct should a Spirit wish to communicate with you; I've also stressed that the Spirit world is not there to tell you what clothes to wear every day. If you go to see a medium, be sure that it is for appropriate reasons. Mediums aren't here to advise you if you should buy a house or marry your girlfriend – I'm sure there are good fortune-tellers and astrologers who can give you an answer there – but it seems that some people will do anything to avoid making that sort of decision for themselves.

Once I was taking a one-to-one sitting for a well-to-do lady but felt from the very beginning that something wasn't quite right. There was someone there in the Spirit world all right, but he seemed curiously reluctant to come through, and I got the sensation that he felt cheated, which was very odd indeed. I explained this to the woman and asked if there was another lady that this Spirit would have been closer to, and she denied it point-blank. The Spirit man gave me a name, and the woman became very agitated and said he should tell *her*, and she'd tell the other woman later, but the man was having none of it.

I couldn't work out what on earth was going on, and the sitting limped to a close because I could feel my own energy going flat. I apologized for not delivering what she had been looking for and said I'd be wasting my time and her own if the Spirit didn't want to pass on information. I tried to explain that sometimes sittings didn't work and that she shouldn't feel upset and so on; maybe it wasn't the right time.

She replied that she was very disappointed that only her brother had come through as he had died recently, yet her mother, who had died years ago, had not bothered. I was a bit surprised by this – it didn't seem very sisterly – but madam went on to say that actually her sister-in-law had been due to have the appointment to see me, but she thought she'd take it instead. Everything I'd said about her brother had been true, but what she really wanted was to hear from her mother as she thought she'd be able to tell her how to get on with her life and guide her to happiness.

No wonder her brother in Spirit hadn't been very pleased! Not only did his sister not really want to hear him, but she'd also snatched his opportunity to communicate with his wife, who was in deep mourning. She'd ruined the chance for the Spirit world to help someone who was truly grieving and may have benefited by contact. When I explained this to her she said she didn't think her sister-in-law had really wanted to come anyway, as she hadn't put up much of a fight. She just can't have realized that people in the rawest stage of grief are often the last to be selfish and demanding.

People will tell all sorts of tales in order to get a slot with a medium, and if they're not genuinely in need, they are only taking appointments from those who are – even if they don't do it as directly as that lady.

Another time when I was working at the SAGB at Belgrave Square I saw a woman who had given the secretary quite a sob story. It's not the medium's job to know the history of a sitter, but the secretaries who take bookings at SAGB are usually very sensitive to those whom they judge need to be seen urgently. I'd got the idea from them that the woman who was seeing me at three was in a bad way and while I was waiting for her I did a sort of preparatory tune-in to Spirit to see if there was someone already there for her.

Nothing came back. This was odd. The woman came in and took a seat and I introduced myself and explained what would happen. I still wasn't getting any of that inner vibration that means the Spirit world is responding. I started mentally to ask my guide why no-one was coming through. Nada. After a few minutes I had to turn to her and tell her that nobody was coming through and we'd have to stop the sitting. I added that my own psychic intuition told me that she hadn't recently lost anyone close to her and she wasn't grieving.

The woman said, 'Oh, no, I'm not in mourning.' She said she'd told the secretary not her own story, but that of her sister-in-law who had just lost her mother. Quite unabashed, she told me she'd swung the appointment so she could have the chance to ask me if I thought she had any potential as a medium herself and if she should join a development group. Can you imagine what sort of medium she'd have made?

A true medium must have the best intentions, and a genuine wish to help the bereaved. If you know that you have to answer to a higher spiritual source, namely your Spirit guide, you're hardly likely to want to delude people for your own gain. People need not only to believe you but also to trust you, and that trust cannot be repaid by making up a nonexistent message or, worse still, ripping them off. I could well imagine that lady telling a sitter all about her own problems and theories but offering precious little consolation for them!

If you want to find a good, trustworthy medium the best place to start is at a reputable Spiritualist church. You can feel your own way there, by attending a few meetings and talking to regular church-goers about what they think of the different mediums who work there. Alternatively, you could attend a few demonstrations and decide if it's for you or not.

Your own common sense is your best guide here, for if you aren't impressed by a particular pundit, it means they are not the person for you. If you feel drawn to one individual it could be because your loved one in Spirit is impressing on you to try to get an appointment with them, and the link you can make will be stronger for it. In the psychic world like attracts like, and some Spirits work better with some mediums than others.

Remember that mediums don't necessarily act or look like 'mediums', wandering around with a sack of crystal balls or an outsize mu-mu. Everyone has different ideas about interior design, and some mediums might feel they work best when surrounded by windchimes and human skulls, while others need a plain old living room and nothing more than a glass of water. It's a matter of personal style, but if you find the atmosphere a bit too Mystic Meg for your liking, it's not the place for you.

Don't just pick someone eenie-meenie-miney-mo from a classified ad in a dodgy magazine with a Post Office box address. Competent mediums are known by reputation in the areas where they operate, and word of mouth will serve you well. Phone lines and readings by post are a bit hit-and-miss and I would never advise someone to spend lots of money seeking out these kinds of operations, as it won't compare to meeting the person in the flesh and getting a good feel for the kind of person they are.

People should know that there are unscrupulous mediums out there, characters who, purely and simply, are out to extort money from the bereaved. One woman in Scotland who billed herself as a famous clairvoyant often told those who came to see her that their family members were about to die, scaring the wits out of them. To add insult to injury, she'd lever hefty sums of money out of them by claiming that she had the power to alter the very same future events she'd just 'predicted' if they'd only come back for a second sitting and shell out more cash.

This was the giveaway. A genuine medium might ask for a fee, but never on the grounds that your Spirit friend could only tell you scraps of information at a time, and that you'd have to come back for the next instalment. A good and decent medium will try and help you there and then to the best of their abilities, and you'll only have to listen to the content of their message to tell if they are for real or not.

Before they even tune into Spirit you should pick up clues as to what sort of operation they are running. They should explain clearly what will happen during the sitting. They will not ask you for any information about yourself or the person you are seeking – pumping you for facts beforehand is a bit of a give-away. They should never guarantee that they'll find the person you want and will let you know quickly if they cannot make a connection. You should never have to sit through a full half hour or even an hour of a medium waffling on about things that mean absolutely nothing to you. A good medium will in turn be sensitive enough to know that they've got the wrong person straight off.

The communication is a three-way process – between yourself, the medium and your Spirit loved ones, and you must be fully involved. You can ask for more clarification too; this is better by far than just nodding and trying to stretch scraps of information together by mere willpower. It's important too that you ask them this before the end of the session when they have tuned out and the connection is broken – they don't know any more than they are told by the Spirits at the time. The information you are looking for may be lost.

The Spirits who come through will make every effort to make themselves describable in a way that enables you to recognize them. It might be the case that some messages come from family members who are not so familiar to you, but overall the main communicators should be known to you. If you're not sure, stop the sitting; the medium should accept this.

Don't sit and concentrate on one person to try and force them to come through and talk. Just relax and ask clearly in your mind before you start if it's possible for them to come, and then leave the rest to Spirit. Too much struggle on your part can block the communication because it might not be what you are desperately thinking you want.

You need to be open and honest to help the medium too, and that's not the same as volunteering all kinds of information about your life. You can trust without being gullible. I've seen plenty of people whip off their wedding rings before a sitting, or sit there defiantly with their arms folded, ready to do battle. A private sitting can be a very emotional time, but there is no need to be afraid of what will happen. You'll know when a Spirit is in contact as you will be left feeling positive and optimistic, not scared or freaked out. Occasionally a sitter does seem to be beyond help, though, but not because the Spirits fail them; these people pretty much let themselves down before I can even get started tuning in.

Even when the Spirits do come through, if the recipient isn't willing to hear what they have to say or aren't open to a life-altering experience, it won't do much good. I once had a man turn up to my flat demanding that I help him. I assured him I'd sort out a private sitting later in the week, but he refused to leave my doorstep. He didn't apologize once for the intrusion, and I could sense that he had no intention of leaving. I had friends visiting at the time, but rather than argue with him, I said I would try.

I led him into one of the bedrooms, sat him down and tried to tune in. I didn't have high hopes because the pushy attitude he gave off didn't seem conducive to Spirit contact to me. Still, someone came through, and I began, 'There is a lady in the Spirit world called Kathleen who makes me aware that she passed very quickly to the other side.'

He cocked his head to one side, sceptically. 'Is there?' I didn't like the way he was taking things and started to lose the plot a little. 'Can you just tell me if you know of someone of this name who died like this, sir?' 'Maybe,' he deadpanned. By now I was annoyed, and determined that he would have his proof, having bullied his way to a reading! It's never good for a medium to have this mind-set, but I'd started, so I'd damn well finish. In any case my Spirit guides were adamant that the message needed to reach this man.

'You are not coping well with your wife's death, she tells me. In fact, you are making life miserable for your family. They've tried hard to help you and all you have done is to sit around believing that you are the only person who has been hurt by her passing.' *Now* he looked angry, but I could also make out beneath that a deep-rooted sadness. I continued.

'You have a son and a daughter and you have been behaving selfishly toward them, Kathleen tells me. You have attempted to take your own life and both of them are distraught because of your actions.' At this point, astonishingly, the man put his hands over his face and burst into tears. I didn't think a pat on the back from me could have helped him more than the home truths that the Spirit world wanted to give him, so I carried on.

'Your wife died two years ago and you have never accepted it; she cannot move on until she feels that you are ok and her children are in a better state of mind. She wants you to know that she did not die to hurt you and that she knows how sad you have been, but it is time for you to carry on living your life.' He cried through this and through all the other messages that came through in that very short sitting. He told me he had tried to kill himself several times and that he knew his son just wouldn't recognize how great his loss had been. He conceded that he had been upsetting his daughter but he also reckoned she was too busy with her own life and that he was now being left out by both of them. Neither of them could understand, as far as he was concerned.

I wasn't surprised now at how stern his wife had been.

He was using his grief to get attention and turning it against those two people closest to him who felt the loss of Kathleen as acutely as he did. Worse, he was pitting them against each other by insinuating that neither of them cared for him any more. I'd had enough of him by now and would have liked to get back to my guests, but I stayed another full hour listening to his problems.

Finally he decided it was time to go home and I walked him to the door with a sense of relief. His parting shot as I waved him off was, 'Do you really believe in all this afterlife stuff? Was that really Kathleen who was talking to you?' I had nothing to say to that, so he announced, 'I don't think anything can help me. They're not suffering the way I am – they look pretty happy sometimes. My son has even gone on holiday with his mates!' He added that this was a disgraceful thing to do, and that the boy's mother was probably turning in her grave at the thought. He didn't say thank you or apologize for taking up my time, either.

As I shut the door I thought he was probably right, he probably *would* never be happy again. All I could envisage when I thought of him was a blackness – a gaping hole like an abyss, and I couldn't imagine that that would ever be filled.

CHAPTER ELEVEN

Messages of Love

Messages of Love

There can be another sad coda to a private sitting, and it's the worst-case scenario for any medium. Someone comes to you desperate for help and when you try and reach the other side for them you get nothing but a radio silence. Thankfully this hasn't happened to me many times over the years, but there is nothing to be done about it when it does crop up.

The only thing to do is to be frank with your sitter and tell them what has happened. It may be that the Spirit is just unable to get through, or that the 'signal' is too weak to work well. It may be that I'm not the right medium for the message. I have no intention of making things up just to jolly along the person sitting opposite me and I'm sure they'd see straight through me if I did.

Several years ago I gave a sitting to a woman whose daughter had been murdered, and who was desperate to see a medium to see if she could get any answers. The girl had been thirteen years old, and there seemed to be no motive to her killing – she had not been robbed or raped, but was brutally attacked and killed when she was out walking one day. At the time her mother saw me the murder was still unsolved.

The mother was gaunt where she had obviously been beautiful; you could see that she was stunning, but it was as though someone had scraped all the flesh from her face. She had clearly been in hell.

I wanted to help, and I sat there with my eyes closed, concentrating all my energy on the Spirit world. I heard nothing. My guides didn't have anything for me. The woman asked anxiously if she ought to try to relax more, and I started to tense up too. After five or ten minutes I had to admit defeat, and, loathe as I was to let her down, tell the woman that I wasn't getting anything.

She instantly blamed herself, saying, 'Am I wanting it too much?' I could only shake my head and tell her, 'Either I'm not the right person or this isn't the right time.' She didn't look too convinced, but thanked me and left. I sat for a long time wondering why on earth I hadn't got a message for her, and feeling helpless.

She did get a communication in the end though, from the late great Ivy Scott, who was in her nineties at the time. It was a brilliant, uplifting message too, full of pieces of evidence. It only came through after the murder trial, oddly enough. Perhaps the girl's mother had been too angry and full of revenge when she saw me, and somehow the girl hadn't been able to get near her. But then again, I have given communications to people who were so distraught they could barely function. I'll never know, but I'm glad Ivy was able to give that poor woman some release from her sorrow, and I hope she is in a far better place mentally now.

At demonstrations I have had to stand up in front of a packed hall of people, all with different needs and all at different stages of grief, and had to apologize and say that nothing is coming through for any of them. When it's happened on other occasions, people have asked anxiously if maybe the reading was too soon, as their relative died only weeks previously, but I've known Spirit people come through when they have been gone a bare few hours.

I've come to reason that these 'no shows' are not a failure of Spirit, but rather of mediumship. Sometimes it just doesn't work. Sometimes there is a sort of interference or conditions surrounding me or the people I am trying to help which prevent the Spirit world making contact. That only seems natural.

I have known people who got no response to receive a message or help some time later – even years later, but as with everything in mediumship, it is best left to the higher Spirits to know their reasons for this. If they show me nothing, then I have nothing.

If you are looking to understand how we communicate with the Spirit world I think that the most important lesson to learn is that, just because someone is a medium, it doesn't mean they're a god or an oracle. They don't know better than everybody else, and they certainly can't solve all your problems. We'd have the world sorted pretty quick if that were true! We can only tell you what the Spirits want you to know.

It's another problem altogether if the sitter doesn't want to receive a message. Usually someone's behaviour is a giveaway, and if it looks like I'm about to pass on a communication that's going in a direction they don't want it to, they try to divert me. This puts me in a dilemma, because obviously the Spirits want to speak to them about it. If this happens, I have to go back to the Spirits and mentally ask them to try another way of gently approaching the subject.

When the sitter just clams up totally and says they don't know what I'm talking about, I have to give up and leave it entirely to the Spirits. They will find another way of getting the message across, through synchronicity or impressing themselves on their loved one's mind.

It's often understandable that people don't want to accept evidence – it might be a public demonstration, and the information is private. I once assured a man at a Spiritualist church that his father had been with him when he was picking up a prescription that last week, and he strenuously denied it, looking very uncomfortable. Afterwards he came up to me and confided that he had indeed been picking up some medication – Viagra! He didn't particularly want his wife who was sitting beside him to find out, though!

It's difficult to have a message rejected, because as a medium you know 110% that it's true. A sense of something that's not quite frustration runs through you from Spirit. Now I always ask three times when someone rejects a piece of evidence. They may say no, then no again, then finally agree that it's true. I also ask people to keep something I've told them in mind, as it may happen in the future instead. It can take a while for that sort of confirmation to show up, but plenty of people have taken the trouble to find me again and tell me that the message came true.

Once when I was doing a TV programme I told a woman that I had her father and his friend Alec with me. And she denied flat out that he'd ever had a friend called Alec. 'Oh, yes, he did,' I said, 'and he's showing me a photograph. He wants you to go home and find it. It's in the second drawer down in the dresser in your room.'

She said, 'That's not true. There's no such photo. I know for a fact it's not there.' More things came through from the father, but the daughter wouldn't budge, and in the end I had to say, 'OK, you don't have to accept it. Please do me a favour, though, and look for that picture.' The TV researchers went home with her that night and, lo and behold, there in the drawer was a photo of her father and a friend, and written on the back was 'Eric and Alec'.

For a medium, knowing that a message is true and being able to give lots of personal information to a total stranger isn't the same as knowing everything about their lives. We're just passing on things we're being told. That doesn't stop a lot of people assuming that we know everything, so they might as well confess everything anyway. I've lost count of the number of times people have been compelled to tell me all kinds of things that I really didn't want to know, and that had nothing to do with the sitting! Their Spirit friends or family probably know it all anyway, so there's no point in telling the messenger too.

I suppose that as they've just experienced the death of a loved one they are thinking over their *own* life, and once they've started unburdening themselves to someone they can't stop. A private reading ends up being a confessional, and when they're done they somehow feel like they've left it with me. For me it feels like way too much information, particularly as it's most often stuff to do with sex!

I've been working for so long that I think I've had every question imaginable thrown at me, and I'll try and answer more of the commonest here, beginning with a rather silly one that seems to be the first thought that pops into some people's heads when they realize that their Spirit loved ones are still with them.

I'd finished a sitting with a lady in her thirties on one occasion and relayed to her many details from her father in the Spirit world, who had given her evidence by bringing up things that had happened since he passed. I thought the hour had gone well, but was surprised to see the woman looking agitated. She'd been out with her husband the previous night in a bar that was a favourite old haunt of her father, and he'd told her that he had 'been' there with them.

Suddenly she burst out, 'I hope he left us after that and didn't see what we did when we got home!' and I saw what the problem was. It was all I could do to reassure her that the Spirits don't spy on us in our most intimate moments. Yes, they are with us, but why would they want to turn Peeping Tom? Thoughts of sex and sense pleasure are, as I always point out, only relevant to this physical world, and don't concern the Spirits. I'm sure they have better things to do.

I've given thousands of messages in all sorts of detail, but I can honestly say I've never given one that featured a Spirit reporting on someone's sexual activities. Mind you, there was a time when I got a message all wrong and left a young lady in London completely bamboozled.

It was a Saturday afternoon and I was working at the SAGB

again, waiting for my second appointment of the day and in walked a very glamorous young lady. She sat down and I checked that she understood what would happen and then began to contact the Spirit world to see who was there for her. It didn't take long to get through to a woman who said she was the young lady's grandmother, Rose, who had died of cancer five years earlier. The young woman accepted this information and we continued merrily with the next twenty minutes of messages from Rose. All seemed well, and my subject seemed happy to be reunited with her nan.

Then I mentioned that Nan knew that her granddaughter had found herself a new job, and that she was watching over her. I was in full flow, pleased to be delivering this comforting information, and added that Nan was glad that the work was helping financially and getting her back on her feet again. On and on I went, then I noticed that the young lady looked aghast. 'Well, I never!' she said, in a broad south London accent.

She still looked puzzled when the sitting finished, as though she was still trying to process what had happened. People often look like that after receiving a message, so I asked if she was ok, and she told me she was and had enjoyed herself, only it was a lot to take in. I smiled and saw her out and didn't give it a second thought.

When I'd finished all my appointments for the day I joined

some of the other mediums for a bite to eat at a local pub. One of my colleagues went to the bar to put in our order for food and I could see her chatting to a little crowd of women who were gathered there. Something amusing was said, because pretty soon they were all laughing uproariously.

My friend could barely get back to our table, she was laughing so hard. 'You'll never guess!' she gasped, and we had to wait till she could get the words out and tell us the joke. It happened that one of the ladies at the bar was Rose's granddaughter, and though she'd told everyone that all the things I'd told her were quite true, what I hadn't realized was that her new job was as a prostitute! She'd been dumbstruck at the thought of her old nan keeping an eye on her while she was at work! And as for getting back on her feet...

I had to go over and dig myself out of that one – of course that wasn't what Rose had meant, not literally – but when I tried to explain her granddaughter just laughed again and told me her nan was a bit of a girl herself and it would have been just like her to say something like that to make everyone crack up. She said she didn't mind, as Rose was probably keeping a lookout for her from the other side. I suppose that's one way of looking at it!

As for the big questions, I can only answer those from my own experience – I don't have any more right to understand life's mysteries than the next man in the street. I'll always try and do what I can to help people and give them advice that seems common sense. As for 'What or who is God?' – well, I'm sorry, but I'm still looking for that one myself. And no, I can't tell if your husband is having sex with another woman – that's not a place I want to go in my mind!

Some mediums do lose the plot and think of themselves as spiritual leaders and draw vulnerable people to them in a way that makes me think of cults. It's a very, very dangerous situation. It might begin with the medium having a genuine spiritual experience, but instead of accepting it, they are scared and turn it into something far more fantastical that never happened.

They think they're channelling Jesus or Buddha, and you've got to wonder what sort of mind-set lies behind someone who feels the need to 'be' a figure like that. Obviously it's really something they've unconsciously made up themselves, but because they need to think that it's really God or a religious leader, they're splitting their own minds in two. And that's when things really go pear-shaped.

There's a huge difference between a medium and a true spiritual teacher. A medium is not a guru or a speedy cure-all. A medium is only human. They enable messages of comfort and hope to pass back to us from the Spirit world but it's up to the recipient to figure out their meaning. It's my own understanding that we must all learn from our experiences in life and in ourselves. That's where the answers to our problems lie if we want to go and look for them. The Spirits might point the way, but they're indicating the solution that we have within us, and not the answer to some profound cosmic puzzle.

CHAPTER TWELVE

A Celebration of Life

A Celebration of Life

When I started out as a medium I never intended to end up officiating at funerals, but now I find that I've lost count of the number I've helped to organise. The very first was for my mentor Mrs Primrose. She had left instructions for a particular minister to conduct the ceremony, but he was out of the country and her daughter May called and asked if I could step in at the last minute. I felt that I could hardly say no, and thought in my innocence that a funeral service, even if it was for such an important figure in my life, couldn't be much different to taking a normal Sunday service in the Spiritualist church. That was something I was used to and I'd never had any problem with it.

So I was a bit thrown when I woke on the morning of the funeral stark, staring terrified. I couldn't believe I couldn't hold myself together. My thoughts were all over the place and when I tried to write notes for the order of service using May's rundown of her mother's life, with all the important points highlighted, I couldn't seem to take anything in. There is something awful about trying to sum up a person's life in the twenty or thirty minutes before the committal in a crematorium, that doesn't seem right.

I'd spoken before large crowds as a medium but nothing could have prepared me for the wave of feelings that comes off a congregation of people at a funeral. I was thankful that I had the pulpit to lean on – it also had the advantage of concealing my trembling knees from everyone who was looking up expectantly at me. The crematorium was packed with members of Mrs Primrose's family, some of whom never knew her as a medium or spiritual teacher. There were masses of her friends and associates from the Spiritualist movement too, all waiting for me to start.

I'd left all my notes in the car, of course. I couldn't really excuse myself and nip out to get them, so I knew I'd landed myself right in it and would have to wing things. My mind was blank as I began by thanking everyone on behalf of Mrs Primrose's family for coming and paying their respects. After that I went into tuned-in medium mode and spoke totally spontaneously, somehow remembering everything which the family had asked me to mention, and I was later told it all sounded very professional and calm.

As I was standing at the door shaking the hands of the mourners one by one, I remember thinking that I'd got away with it this time, but I'd never do it again as long as I lived. The thing is, it seems that every time in my life I get through a public ordeal like that and swear it's the last time, it seems to come right back at me – with a vengeance.

In the year after Mrs Primrose's funeral I was asked to preside over no fewer than six, and each time I wanted to turn them down and pass them on to a minister, but each family asked for me personally and it's extremely difficult to refuse people in that very low stage of grief. I began to notice how important a funeral is to a family, even in that numb state, and how, if conducted properly, it can help them move onto the next stage of bereavement a little more easily.

They are under great strain at the time, trying to think how to best sum up their loved one's life and give them a fitting tribute, and often feel totally helpless. I always offered them a practice to do – the same one I use whenever someone close to me has died. I offer up a prayer to the Spirit of the dead person and pray for them to advance in the Spirit world. For a Spiritualist this is common practice, but it had never occurred to me that others didn't do this.

I always included it in the funeral services I conducted, and people kept coming up to me at the end and asking if it was right for them to carry on with the prayers after the funeral as they had felt a connection to the Spirit of the deceased by doing the practice. I can always assure them that it is of course ok, as it would genuinely help their loved one on the other side to progress and it would in time help the Spirit to communicate with his or her living relatives. It would keep the line of mental connection open.

Ever since that first funeral a sort of pattern emerged where everything that could go wrong, did, and I always seemed to be operating under some sort of handicap. In some cases I wonder if the Spirit is having a good laugh at my expense. If the mishaps occurred once or twice I'd put it down to coincidence, but when it happens time after time I do wonder who or what is behind it.

One service almost went horribly wrong when the music started up for the committal. The family had provided a tape of the mother's favourite song to be played – Diana Ross singing *Amazing Grace*. As the casket began to move and the song kicked in, I realized I'd picked up the wrong cassette: the opening chords of the Clash's *London's Burning* were ringing out round the crematorium. Luckily the man at the hi-fi had the tape speedily ejected before it could get to the chorus, and the organist improvised another version of *Amazing Grace* instead.

On another occasion I was taking the service for a woman who was the sister-in-law of a close friend and had died very tragically at a young age, leaving behind her husband and children. I really wanted this occasion to be remembered by the family as a day of celebration of her life and had painstakingly put together a fitting programme, which took me days to fine-tune.

The night before, my mouth was painful and I realized it was my new denture giving me gip – it replaced the incisors on either side of my front teeth, and was rubbing my gums and causing a sore.

I took the plate out and put it in a glass by my bed so that my mouth could heal. The crematorium was quite a distance from my home so I went to bed early, setting my alarm carefully. I knew the service backwards, I just needed some sleep and I'd be fine.

When I woke up I felt my gums with my tongue and they seemed to have healed nicely. I turned to the glass on my bedside table and it slowly dawned on my foggy early-morning brain that the denture had vanished. This was exactly the kind of thing smart alecks tell me I should be psychic about, but before I could blame the other side I realized to my horror what had happened.

My springer spaniel Meg leapt onto the bed and gave me an unusually toothy grin … After I'd wrestled her new chew-toy off her, the day was saved only by denture cleaning fluid and superglue. It didn't look too bad, but every time I pronounced an 's' I let out a high pitched whistle, and I caught a few people at the back of the room giving me very puzzled looks indeed!

Funny stories aside, with each funeral service I have taken I have learned something new about grief, probably because it represents such an important stage in the process. It is the point at which reality steps in and brings home to us that someone we love is not going to be a part of our physical world any more, and the family's need for hope is overwhelming. Learning that they will be reunited with their loved ones and will be able to be spiritually and mentally in contact with them can bring them great comfort at a harrowing time.

The relatives of a friend of an old work colleague asked me to officiate at his funeral after he'd died suddenly of a heart attack at the age of fifty-five. I knew him and his family to be resolute atheists, but so many people had sent their heartfelt condolences that his wife asked if I could fashion some sort of non-religious tribute to the man, to give an account of his life at the committal.

I set about carefully constructing a farewell service that would not include hymns, prayers or anything else which might resemble a religious ceremony, but I could tell that his wife was struggling as she didn't want to think that everything they had had together had just been wiped out with his shocking death. She needed answers. I spent a lot of time with other members of the family, gathering stories about the man's life, and I could feel that they all, at some point, wanted to ask me about life after death, and whether, despite his atheism, he would go on in the hereafter.

As I stood before them on the day I was sorely tempted to ask people to pray for the man to progress in the afterlife, but couldn't as it would have meant disrespecting his family's wishes. During the committal, as the coffin was moving slowly through the heavy velvet curtains, his wife began to scream his name out loud, over and over again. She ran to me and called out blindly, 'Where is he? Tell me where he is! He can't have left me!'

Her children leapt up to hug her and gently bring her back to her seat, terrified she'd break down again. When the ordeal was over I tried to go up to the family and tell them that if any of them wanted to talk to me about anything I was there for them and they only had to call. It was painful to see them as they all looked lost and defeated. Maybe they thought that even to think about an afterlife would be a betrayal of their father's beliefs. I felt powerless to help them and yet knew exactly what the questions were that were rolling round and round their minds. The service, at their own request, had given them no answers.

A funeral is a final chance to give something to your loved one, out of sentiment and as testament to your love for them. It is very important for the bereaved to be given a chance to display their feelings and special connections to the deceased in a way that will thank them for being a special part of their lives. You should put as much energy as you can into it, allowing for your grief at that time. When it is over, there isn't that much to occupy yourself with apart from thinking about your loved one and coming to terms with your sadness, but if the ceremony went well you can look back on it and say, 'I did the best thing I could for him. He had a good sendoff.'

The funeral also has the very important function of priming that 'jewel box' of memories of the deceased that will ultimately bring healing to the grieving. From then onwards, you begin to look for the departed in the more subtle state of mind through memory. Memories come to the fore, reiterating that bond between the loved one who has passed over and those left behind. I learned an important lesson about the way to conduct this from Reverend Miller, who works in one of the worst-off areas of Glasgow, and who presided over the funeral of one of my aunts.

My aunt had asked for me to join Reverend Miller in the service, and he let me, though as he said, 'I don't normally encourage this sort of thing because family find it difficult to speak at funerals, but I do know who you are and I understand you want to do this.' I'm glad he let me see him work at first hand. I have never seen someone take that twenty minutes before the committal to make such a beautiful, full summary of a person's life.

He went back over every decade of my aunt's life, telling stories about her at every age, so that everyone in the room was drawn into the reminiscence. Those who had known her only as an old woman learned what she had been like as a teenager and those who had known her in childhood found out what she had achieved as an adult. The detail was essential to involve everyone and fill in the gaps they had in their picture of her, the hardships and the triumphs, as a friend, workmate, lover and mother.

It brought her back to life, and we could all see what an amazing person she was, and how she'd affected everyone around her. Reverend Miller then took her death as a point of ascendancy – a promotion that crowned the description he'd just given of her life. It was wonderfully uplifting, and left everyone thinking of her and wanting to know more from other people about those different parts of her time in this world.

Now I take my cue from Reverend Miller when working with a family over funeral arrangements. The service which I prepare for people is based on what I have heard the close relatives say when I ask them to go through their most important memories, and that is more beneficial than any practised sermon I could deliver.

I try gently to prompt them to look through the cloud of sadness which hangs over them and guide them back to the living memories of their loved one that cemented their relationship, whether these be a song, a poem or a funny story. Hopefully I can then do justice to those recollections and let everyone there on the day experience the life force of that person and not just think about a light that has gone out.

It is so important that people come out with the things they want included, as otherwise if they leave the service thinking that they should have said something, or contributed a reading, the knowledge that they didn't adds another layer of depression and helplessness to their grief. They need to feel part of the final sendoff for someone they loved deeply. The readings need not be religious, unless they say something in particular about the deceased and had true significance for them.

I also take Reverend Miller's advice about who does the readings. You should not speak if you are unable to do so. I will always remember one family who had three relatives to speak – one read from the dead person's favourite book, one from the Bible and one spoke from the heart. Every one of them ended up being overcome when they stood up to speak, and choked up completely.

You cannot underestimate the way that you will react to all the emotions that are flying around during the service, as even the most composed speaker can find themselves struggling for words. Sometimes people just end up essentially weeping before a crowd of their nearest and dearest, rather than saying the important words they had prepared.

People who choose not to use notes often have the worst time, just going over how much they love and miss their loved one. Everybody knows and sympathizes with this, but it focuses them on a loss, not a life. Often it's just easier to get someone else to read, and though it's better if they are family, it's not necessary.

I've certainly found when I've officiated at the funerals of people whom I was very close to in life that it was extremely difficult to remain unmoved myself. Even though I knew that they had moved on to the spiritual life, like everyone else I still experience the loss of the physical life. As a sensitive I am also very aware of the strong sensation of sadness which comes from all the assembled mourners, and need to try and mentally remove myself from that if I am to deliver a good service. I have also sometimes experienced the Spirit person whose funeral it was watching over the proceedings.

When I was asked by my dear friend Effie, some weeks before she passed, if I would take her funeral service, I had no option but to say yes. I didn't want to do it. Effie had been battling cancer for five years, and was very clear about the fact that she was dying and that she had to help her family and friends deal with that. She was the salt of the earth, a spiritual healer who worked as a cleaner and who wrote amazing poetry. She had more kindness and compassion in the tip of her little finger than most people manage in their entire body. No matter how bad her illness got, she always found time to talk to others on her hospital ward when they were afraid. She had plenty of down-to-earth wisdom to share. It could really be said that she touched the lives of everyone who met her.

She'd begun to prepare her own service and would ask me to go over to her house so she could instruct me what to do. Every time I popped round she made light of things and always had me in stitches with some of her ideas, and the reasons she wanted these things were even funnier. It was a very strange situation to be in.

The very day before she died she explained to me that she wanted people to be happy for her because she would be beyond suffering. She was adamant that she be remembered by her sons and grandchildren for the way she had lived her life and for always trying to find joy in a situation. As I left she gave me a cassette and told me it was set at a track that she wanted played during her committal, and told me strictly that I must not listen to it beforehand. This didn't bother me, but the wicked smile on her face gave me cause for concern. I knew she loved Elvis, and I was pretty sure we were going to end up with *Blue Suede Shoes*, or, worse, *Return to Sender*!

The following day, Effie went back home to Spirit, and she had that same wicked smile on her face when she passed.

A week later I was standing at the front of the crematorium looking out at a sea of people from all walks of life which filled every bench, the aisles, the back of the room and extended out through the doors and into the corridor. Effie had been so loved by so many people that the turnout alone was a tribute. Each reading, each piece of music and each hymn she chose was dedicated to her family and pointed them to a particular memory of her life.

People chuckled as the stories rolled out. There was a poem she'd written and a piece about how atrocious her doctor was – look, Effie said, at the evidence! The doctor, who was one of the consultant oncologists in a big Glasgow hospital, was there roaring with laughter along with everyone else. I read a poem I'd written too, when she was entering her final stages.

Every morning when she left for work at 5am, Effie would feed the birds outside her house and talk to the tree there, the only one on the street: 'Morning, Tree. Those bloody children have been pulling your branches again. Nice day, though. Right, Tree, that's me off to work.' In the evening when she came home she'd stop to pass the time of day with the tree again: 'Evening, Tree. Well, what a day I've had. How was your day? Still, I'd better be off up the road as I've got fish to fry and my sons are here tonight. See you in the morning.'

I don't usually write poetry, but this one came out of nowhere and it was all in broad Glaswegian and about the tree and the seasons, with the story of Effie's life woven through it.

She loved it, and couldn't get over the fact that I'd been listening to everything she'd been saying for all those years! So the poem made it into the funeral with Effie's good grace.

I did make one addition though, as I thought that Effie's funeral might be *too* funny, and that people would need some time for quieter reflection. I found an opera singer to perform *I think that I should never see a poem lovely as a tree*. As we all stood listening to the beautiful music ring out I was suddenly aware of Effie's Spirit being near me, and she was saying, 'Oi, son! *I* planned this funeral.'

It all went according to Effie's plan, though, with everyone being uplifted. And the committal music? I'd told her sons their mother had made me promise to play the cassette, and they said, 'We know it's Elvis.' The man operating the tape machine had asked me if I knew what it was, and I said I had no idea. 'That is not a good thing,' he said sternly, and I had to try to explain what an exceptional woman Effie had been. So there I was standing in the pulpit, braced for the worst, warning everybody that, well, they knew Effie …

And it was Elvis, but he was singing *How great Thou art*. There was barely a dry eye in the house. I should have trusted Effie – we didn't need the opera singer to provide that moment, Effie had it all sorted. It was part of her nature to take the sting out of painful things in people's lives when it was in her considerable powers. When they thought about her goodbye, it would bring a smile to their faces instead of leaving them sad.

I don't advise everyone to go out to Elvis, but I do advise them to want to be remembered for who they were and to leave the door open for good memories to follow when their families think of them. It doesn't have to be a laugh a minute to be uplifting, that was just Effie's way, but real, true sentiment will always have that positive effect. And the resonance of that experience will continue through the lives of those who were there to see their friend off.

Music has a particular power, as every time you hear that song in the future, your mind will go back to the one who passed over. The famous medium Doris Stokes had *Wish me luck as you wave me goodbye* and I bet I'm not the only one who can't hear it without picturing her! More soberly, when my cousin died he chose a U2 song, *One*, and even though I never knew him that well in life, whenever I hear that song I send him thoughts.

A song is so evocative that it becomes like a signature tune, and it's a tremendously powerful thing to say, 'I want to remember you by this song, because this is what it meant to me.' It's part of your 'jewel box' of memories.

The funeral is not just for you, but for the Spirit who is celebrated too. It's a kind of appraisal of a person's life that they can take with them into the next world and begin to progress. It doesn't seem right to let sentiment paint too rosy a picture of how they were, as it's far better to be honest if you are going to do justice to a real life. People's lives are a complicated mix of good and bad, and the Spirits will need to look at both as they try to progress.

I do think Spirits always see their funerals. That's why it's so sad when a funeral cannot take place because the body could not be found; everyone, Spirit and mourners, is left with a sense of dislocation and mystery. The Spirit will find its way home, though, if there's the presence of their loved ones thinking together about them.

From the point of view of the Spirit person, I am sure that the sendoff and the love which is displayed by a family does help them in the Spirit world. First, it is their birth into a new life and just as people shower love on a newborn child when they first enter this life and try to make them feel secure in their new surroundings, then the love we feel as we depart can give us security in our new Spirit life.

I have made contact with many, many Spirits who remark on how they felt lifted on entering Spirit, because of the effect which their life had on the people they connected to here. I have also become aware from those Spirit communicators that, when their loved ones gather at a funeral or remembrance of their life, they are given a boost as it were in the Spirit world and that when we pray for their advancement in the Spirit world, that it does actually lift them spiritually away from some of the darker moments of their former life.

Having to accept this new situation and feeling separated from the comforts and love of the world we have left, the Spirit body has to adjust and make sense of the love and action carried out in the former physical existence. It is much easier to adjust if you know that the effects of your behaviour as a person in the physical world caused love and that people are remembering what good you did.

Often people incorporate very, very personal gestures which are extremely important. One mother told me she dressed her son in a Rangers football shirt, because it brought back such a lovely memory. She'd got one for him when he was thirteen and he'd started to cry because he couldn't believe that his parents had bought it for him as they barely had the money to afford it. She said it was 'the one thing I wanted to give him in the next life.' It was so important for her as a mother, and also could have been a piece of evidence for him to give her from the other side.

The strangest things can become a connection to the afterlife, as bizarre as that may sound. I know a couple whose boy died in an accident just before the family were due to go on holiday, and the father tucked his passport, his plane ticket and some foreign currency into the casket with him. I wasn't aware of this but when I gave them a reading the son mentioned having the things, and said, 'It will help.' It meant the world to his parents, even without that message – just making that gesture which said, 'You are coming on holiday too, and you are with us all the time'.

If you do have the urge to do something like that, you should act on it. Don't be ashamed – there's a reason for that urge. It's from the heart. Do what you want to do, and don't feel inhibited from making that effort. When my cousin Steven died, my Aunt Sylvia took the stance that this was her only chance to have a big celebration for her young son. She would never see him married or have children, so she made his funeral perfect. It became something to plan and to look back on.

One of the things she did was to tie black bows round the necks of Steven's dogs and take them to the funeral too, which some people disapproved of, but which meant so much to her. Steven had loved the dogs and the dogs loved Steven – they'd howled and howled when his coffin was taken from the house. They were part of his life, so it was only fitting that they should be there.

By the same token, don't be persuaded to do something that you know wasn't right. If the type of flowers is important, it's because they are important to you. However, I've seen people get so wrought up because they thought the arrangements weren't exactly right, but on the scale of things a few misplaced peonies aren't much compared to the loss of a loved one. With emotions running high, sometimes people take their distress from one thing and channel it into something that seems trivial instead.

Sometimes it's better not to attend a funeral. If you choose not to go to one, stick to that decision and don't go over it again and again when it's too late. If you believe in Spirit as much as I do, then not going to a funeral will not make you depressed because it is a ceremony for those who need it, and not your only means of access to the Spirit. They know how you feel about them, and you can send prayers for them from anywhere. It matters more what you think about missing the occasion, as your loved one would not want you to beat yourself up about it. If you don't go because you have difficulty facing the thought of death, those in Spirit will see that and understand.

Not going because it wasn't possible is a different thing again – if you're on the other side of the globe or you didn't know it was happening, you have to learn that you were just not meant to be there. The quicker you accept that you can't change that, the quicker you will move on. Again, you can offer thoughts to the deceased from anywhere, and that is what matters.

When my Aunt Sylvia was dying she was very clear that I should go on a holiday I had booked with one of my sons, not realising that that was the week she would slip away. As we chatted in the hospice she told me that this was our time together, and that it meant more than me turning up at the ceremony in a few days time. So I did go away, and on the day of the funeral I went somewhere quiet to think of her and offer some prayers for her Spirit.

One of the things that people agonize over is the question of whether or not to take young children to the service. This depends so much on the child. If it is their first experience of death, they will only be terrified. They have no idea about their own emotions and are surrounded by adults who are themselves distraught. The very worst thing would be to see a loved one disappear in a box into a hole in the ground.

It sounds like a really silly thing to say here, but kids should have hamsters! That way they have a first take on death, at the poor old hamster's expense, and though it's only a small thing, it's something that will help them build the emotions they need to cope with something far greater later in life.

The funeral is a big day both for people in the physical world and for those now in the Spirit world, as we travel part of the journey into death with our loved ones. We send them on a beautiful journey with our best wishes and memories. It shows in a very real way how the stages of our life aren't permanent, and that we are in a state of change. It is a reminder to us in this form that we are mortal for a time and that our hopes and dreams of a continued existence are much more subtle, lying outside our five human senses.

We can learn that the feelings we have and the thoughts which are invisible to others in this world become the place where we look for God and higher powers and through which we may reach out for a finer existence. It truly lies within us.

CHAPTER THIRTEEN

Bringing Comfort

Bringing Comfort

When I was a child growing up in Glasgow, I always knew when someone in the street had died, because my mum's big black handbag would come out. Then she'd take a piece of paper and a pen and march from door to door with the handbag, collecting donations from the neighbours for the family that had lost someone. They gave what they could afford – a pound, half-a-crown or a bob. On the paper she made a note of each contribution, and when she took the money round to hand it over, she'd give the family the sheet too, so they could see that the whole community was thinking of them.

This was money that they could use to buy a headstone or cover the funeral, or just to tide the household over while they couldn't go out to work. It was like sending a sympathy card that had been signed by everyone. You can't get much from bereavement, but you can find comfort in the knowledge that so many people are thinking of you and wishing you the best. It really was a big deal in our street too, because people didn't have much.

The second thing my mum would do would be to make

food. She'd say to my dad, 'Sammy, you'd better buy a ham hock. Mr So-and-So has died,' and Dad would say, 'Oh eh. Send one of the weens round to the butcher. We're making a pot of soup.' When it was ready she'd carry it round to the Mr So-and-So's house, so his family would have something to eat without worrying about cooking or buying stuff.

It was real practical help. What could be better than that?

The bereaved have been catapulted out of the normal world and it's difficult for them to handle much everyday life; it's very easy for them to end up more and more isolated. It's the job of those around the bereaved to provide that sort of normality by continuing to do the ordinary sort of stuff, like making a pot of soup so they have something to eat.

Trying to help the bereaved can seem a bit like it does when you try to heal someone with a terminal illness; you have so far to go to overcome the grief. That just means you have to make a lot of effort, whether that's to turn up every day and ask if they need help or to try to be as ordinary around them as possible. Trying to bring them back to that ordinariness is better than throwing big hugs or going in armed with platitudes that mean nothing.

The best way to do it is to offer help quietly without over-stepping the mark. The family will let you know when they want space and privacy, directly or indirectly, and you've got to respect that wish.

Neighbours do so little now compared to what happened when I was a child, and I suppose that's partly because we feel so inadequate in the face of grief, and think there's nothing we can do for them. People start to make excuses like, 'I didn't want to intrude,' or, 'I'm sure they'll ask if they want help,' when they're really hoping someone else will step forward and do it for them.

For some the idea of death is just so terrifying that they can't face approaching their friends who are in mourning, almost as though they're afraid of some sort of taint of bad luck by going near them. It's nonsense to think of those people who are hurting so much as being Typhoid Marys who threaten your own family. A small effort for them can cost you so little, but mean so much to them when they finally make it out of their depression.

I don't think many people who have just suffered a loss would turn away a gesture as simple and heartfelt as that pan of soup. One of the only people I do know who refused any help from neighbours was my own mother, again, and she was so determined to be independent that I don't think she let anyone do things for her. Her father lived with us when he was ill, and my dad went in to take him his cup of tea one morning and couldn't wake him. My mum knew at once that he was dead, and she let out a terrible scream – the same as she'd done when she realized her mother had died years earlier.

Us kids all froze, but Mum swung into action, having bare-ly skipped a beat: 'You're sure he's dead? Get a doctor. You,' – to my sister – 'go down and buy two dozen rolls. And you buy blinds. We've got to have blinds, 'cause we've got a priest com-ing. And somebody clean this hoose! You can't let a bloody priest into a dirty hoose!' By the time some of the next-door neighbours came round she was totally composed, and just said, 'We have everything. Everything is fine. You don't need to do anything.' She would have appreciated the fact that they tried, though, and that was what counted.

We did get a sympathy card from the poorest family in the street, and it just said very simply, 'We don't have much but what we have is yours for the taking.' I remember crying about that when I was a little boy, it was such a powerful thing to say. It really touched my mother too. Those words were more valuable than anything that household could afford to give. The card made that thought a gesture.

One gesture that we do seem to make now is to leave a card and a bunch of flowers at a house or an accident site, and that's a great thing to do. It's a token which marks how much we cared, and visual proof for the bereaved family of how many people are thinking of them and their loved one. Reading letters and cards that people send in the wake of a death with their memories of the one who has passed is also a good comfort. They can see just how the deceased fitted into everyone's lives and made a difference. There's good medicine in these simple sentiments.

I've heard all kinds of stories of people mishandling others' grief. My friend Ros lost her eighteen-year-old son in a car accident and was, obviously, devastated. After a couple of weeks of enduring a living hell at home, her instincts told her it was time to try to get herself at least physically out of a rut, and do something to occupy her mind and stop it turning in on itself. So she went back to her job in a bank.

Try to imagine how she felt on her first day back when one of her customers took one look at her and said, 'You've obviously gotten over the death of your son fast.' Outwardly, Ros tried to act as though this thoughtless comment hadn't affected her, but inside she was mortified. She began to question her own decision to return to work, and wonder if others were judging her like this lady. Thankfully she had the presence of mind to follow that first instinct, which was to carry on being as positive as she could and cope as best she could with life while dealing with her terrible loss.

As I hope I've shown so far in this book, everyone will react and behave differently to loss. What matters is what helps them, and not the opinion of others. It is difficult enough to live with the death of anyone we have loved without the added pressure of worrying what people will think of you. There is no fixed period for mourning. Those grieving will let you know when they are feeling more able to face the world.

You can't quantify each individual's grief; it needs to be worked through, and eventually the death has to be accepted if people are to heal and grow in their life. There is nothing to be gained by telling a person who has recently suffered a loss that there are people who have experienced far worse and have come through it, or that their grief does not measure the pain felt by someone else. Often people are far too quick to judge and make statements like, 'It was only an elderly relative they lost so they should be able to get over that ok.' Or, 'It has been six months now, you would think they would be better adjusted by now.'

It's best always to try to be kind to someone who is suffering and not appear clever and self-righteous as they may be at their lowest. Your kindness may be something which they remember in their dark times, rather than a smug answer that can only make them feel inadequate on top of their sadness.

Even if what I observe in a person is that they appear to be childish or no more than needy in their grief, no good will come from forcing them to get over their loss quickly. The only way you can intervene in this sort of circumstance is if you are a very good friend indeed and can make sure that your own motives aren't selfish.

Death is, in a way, contagious, because your friend has lost a loved one and you probably feel in turn that you have lost your friend. They're not the same person they used to be, and they don't seem to be on the same planet any more. It's hard to reach them, and all but impossible to second-guess how they feel.

It's a different matter if you think they have been so crippled by grief that they are stuck into a damaging pattern of behaviour. If you are truly good friends you should be able to tell them anything, especially that you are worried and think they are falling deeper and deeper into a depression which will only hurt them and those around them.

The bereaved never asked to feel the way they do. It might be the first time they have lost someone, and they have nothing to measure their sadness by. They want to be happy again, don't forget, but it's that nagging emptiness that undercuts everything they now do. If you have nothing positive to put in place of that, don't bother. You can't tell them to get better soon because they're no fun any more – that comes from your own selfishness, not compassion. The key here is showing that you are concerned, and not just giving them a boot and telling them to cheer up because it's about time.

Don't try and overcompensate and take on a different role either, like assuming that you are a far greater friend than you actually are. Your feelings must be genuine too, as phoney emotions won't wash. Very often the absolute best thing you can do is to be there, and maybe not even say anything, but definitely to listen. Offering yourself and your time to your best friend is one of the biggest gifts you can make.

CHAPTER FOURTEEN

Spiritual Joy

Spiritual Joy

In 1995 I travelled to Düsseldorf in Germany to give some private readings and a seminar. I had to work with an interpreter, who was called Christina, because I don't speak the language; I would relay the messages in English and she would translate them straight into German for the sitter.

One day Christina brought a very elderly lady to my hotel room for a reading and introduced her as Helena. They made themselves comfortable opposite me and I began to explain via Christina how everything would work. Helena nodded in agreement and I started to tune into the Spirit world to ask if there was anyone there who needed to reach Helena.

In my mind's eye I could see a young man, tall and handsome, sitting at a table in a dimly-lit café; I described him and Christina told Helena in turn, who looked baffled. She was just opening her mouth to say she didn't recognize this person when I heard a voice call 'Dieter'. She clapped her hands over her mouth and nodded that she knew him.

I asked my Spirit guides to make the link between the name

and the young man and they confirmed that he was indeed Dieter and that he had passed during the Second World War. I closed my eyes and saw a scene unfold – something I rarely do. Usually I hear messages rather than see them played out, but this time it was like watching a film. In that café I could see a beautiful girl sitting opposite Dieter and holding his hands. They got up from the table and went outside to stand together under a streetlight in the snow. I knew that they were in Berlin.

Christina kept checking with Helena that this was true, and she kept nodding. I saw the couple kissing and embracing each other and I could hear and repeat their conversation for Helena. Dieter was saying how much he loved her and that when he came back from the navy they would marry. He took off his glasses, which had a gold frame, and gave them to the woman, telling her to have them melted down for a wedding ring. They stood quietly for a while and then Dieter started to sing and they both laughed and began to dance under the streetlight. When the scene ended I opened my eyes and saw Christina and Helena both in tears. The young woman was obviously Helena. I continued to tell them the message as I heard it.

Dieter said that he was a submariner who died at sea in 1944 and that he had continued to watch over Helena after his death. He said too that he had guided her when she was escaping from Germany at the end of the war. Helena continued to nod, and

Dieter told me about a tiny farmhouse in Holland where he had led her and that he'd known that as she was struggling across Europe she could often feel his presence. He knew that she'd thanked him, even though she had wanted to die when she'd heard he'd been killed. He added that he was glad she still wore his ring, and Helena lifted her right hand to show Christina and me the gold band.

He had come through to communicate with her because he wanted her to know that he was happy that she had found love again, and said that he was in Spirit with her husband, Paul, who had recently died. He told Helena she must not upset herself by going over and over terrible memories of the war and that everyone on both sides had suffered enough loss. He mentioned others she had lost during her life and told her that she must be at peace with herself and know that she was a good person who had been caught up in a horrendous situation, and had to do all she could to save herself.

Her husband Paul then came forward and I heard his voice instead. He passed on a gentle message of love and thanks, promising her that she would never feel lonely as so many of her loved ones were looking on. Then the sitting ended.

Christina, Helena and I all went to have a coffee together to think over what had just happened and Helena told me her story in great detail, and this time Christina translated it for me instead. Everything in the message had been true, and fitted into the tale she told me now. After she met and married Paul she had been unable to forget Dieter, sometimes feeling as though she was betraying her husband when she wondered what her life with her first love might have been like.

She'd also felt that both the men would have been great friends had they met in life, and this thought sustained her. When Paul died suddenly of a heart attack she had felt the need to see a medium so she could have a chance to say a proper goodbye, but the last thing she had expected was for Dieter to come through, and for him to be standing alongside Paul.

This was a true story of love never dying and I think that if we truly love someone neither death nor time has any bearing on it. Dieter had loved Helena passionately but when she had a second chance at family life and happiness he moved on and allowed her that. When she was left bereft after the death of her husband he reappeared to comfort her. There is nothing selfish about real love, and it transcends personality to become healing and nurturing. When people die it is this love which persists and lives on with the Spirit.

Love is the answer to most of the questions people have about Spirit communication. When there is a true bond of love between people, not even death can separate them; true love between people allows them to permeate each other's very being, and makes it possible for the departed to impress messages on their loved ones. Even though grief may make it feel like that bond has been severed, in time when the clouds are parted just enough, the love will come shining through again.

I've often thought that when we experience this kind of love in our world it is indescribable, because it comes from that higher, more spiritual side of our nature – the very part that links us to the life beyond the material. Your love for your partner, your child or your friend gives you a glimpse of what is to come in the next life.

I think this is the greatest lesson that the death of a loved one can teach us. When you find that bond of love that goes beyond this life, you have learned a great spiritual lesson for yourself, which can bear you through any ordeal. While that bond may be distorted by death, or by conflicting emotions like anger or guilt, it truly can never be broken. It's there to teach us about Spirit, and make a bridge between the two worlds.

Our mind is the keeper of all our past experiences, hopes, fears and memories, and it has a higher level that can help us if we let it. It's the very essence of us in Spirit. I believe it's a higher, purer state of mind that we're often afraid to approach because our physical self is so flawed in comparison with our Spirit being, yet everything that we think we are now is nothing to what we will truly become.

Every ordeal, even grief, can be overcome, and nothing is beyond us if we reach out to Spirit, and step up to join it.

Also Available by Gordon Smith

Spirit Messenger

Read Gordon's first book, *Spirit Messenger*, and find out how he became a medium, what has influenced his spiritual development over the years and what it has been like to work with the scientific world.

Full of stories told in Gordon's down-to-earth style, *Spirit Messenger* is the beginning of the journey.

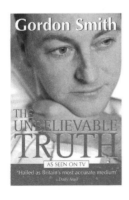

The Unbelievable Truth

In this, Gordon's second book, he answers the questions he is most often asked by the people he meets. Gordon explains how the world of Spirit works, how Spirits communicate; he covers ghosts, hauntings, out-of-body experiences and much more. Ideal for anyone searching for more information on this huge subject area and a perfect accompaniment to *Through My Eyes* and *Spirit Messenger*.

Don't forget you can find out more about Gordon Smith, his life, his work and his upcoming personal appearances by visiting his official website: www.psychicbarber.com